CW00369169

Faith in the
Religion, identity and the public realm
in Britain today

With a Foreword by The Prime Minister, Rt Hon Gordon
Brown MP

Edited by

Zaki Cooper and Guy Lodge

Institute for Public Policy Research

ippr

The Institute for Public Policy Research is the UK's leading progressive think tank, producing cutting-edge research and innovative policy ideas for a just, democratic and sustainable world.

Since 1988, we have been at the forefront of progressive debate and policymaking in the UK. Through our independent research and analysis we define new agendas for change and provide practical solutions to challenges across the full range of public policy issues. ·

With offices in both London and Newcastle, we ensure our outlook is as broad-based as possible, while our international and migration teams and climate change programme extend our partnerships and influence beyond the UK, giving us a truly world-class reputation for high quality research.

Contents

Acknowledgements

The editors would firstly like to thank all the contributors to this collection. At ippr we would like to thank Lisa Harker, Georgina Kyriacou, and Rick Muir. We would also like to thank James Crabtree and Robin Gambles for offering thoughtful comments on earlier drafts of the essays. Finally we would like to thank Sir Trevor Chinn for his generous support of this project and ippr's wider work on faith and politics.

About the contributors

Rt Hon Gordon Brown MP is the Prime Minister.

Zaki Cooper is an inter-faith activist and commentator. He is a Trustee of the Council of Christians and Jews, and a consultant to the Cambridge University inter-faith programme.

Dilwar Hussain is Head of the Policy Research Centre at the Islamic Foundation, Leicester.

Ramesh Kallidai is the Secretary General of the Hindu Forum of Britain.

Michael Kenny is Professor of Politics at the University of Sheffield. He is currently a Visiting Research Fellow at the Institute for Public Policy Research.

Guy Lodge is Head of the Democracy and Power team at the Institute for Public Policy Research. He is also a Visiting Research Fellow in the Department of Politics and International Relations at Oxford University.

Cardinal Cormac Murphy-O'Connor is the Archbishop of Westminster and President of the Bishops' Conference of England and Wales.

Sir Jonathan Sacks is the Chief Rabbi of the United Hebrew Congregations of the Commonwealth.

Dr John Sentamu has been the Archbishop of York since 2005. He is Primate of England and Metropolitan, a member of the House of Lords and a Privy Councillor.

Dr Indarjit Singh OBE is the Director of the Network of Sikh Organisations and editor of the *Sikh Messenger*.

Foreword

By the Prime Minister, Rt Hon Gordon Brown MP

In contrast to claims in previous decades that a decline in formal religious participation would spell a death-knell for religious belonging and belief, faith in Britain today is very much alive and well. At the last Census, more than three-quarters of the population said they belonged to a faith, and – as this collection of essays by faith leaders underlines – people's religious identities go right to the heart of their sense of themselves and their place in society and the world.

Britain, of course, has a strong Christian tradition, but the landscape of our country today is resolutely multi-faith. Time after time in British history, faith communities arriving on these shores have not only integrated and settled into British life but have made extraordinary contributions as well, often in the face of great adversity – and the rich culture, diverse economy and educational, scientific and entrepreneurial standing that Britain enjoys today is a testament to the lasting force for good that they have been.

But the religious leaders writing here do not simply tell the stories of how their communities have shaped and been shaped by British life. Together with ippr's Professor Kenny, they also raise some important questions about what the relationship between faith communities and the state should look like in a multi-faith society. How, for example, can we recognise and value the role of religion in British society without compromising the essential equalities that lie at the heart of the secular state? How can we create space for the voices of religious and secular leaders alike as we debate some of the biggest moral challenges of our day – the impact of climate change and scarce resources, the implications of rapid scientific and medical progress, and the ideological fault lines that rise to the fore in a globalised world? And how can we ensure that different faith groups are all able to contribute to a shared set of British values, rather than viewing diversity as a barrier to a shared and meaningful national identity?

These questions and many others are explored in the pages of this groundbreaking publication – the first of its kind to bring faith leaders together to reflect on the kind of society that, as a nation, we aspire to build. Their answers are not always the same, but one message comes across clearly and consistently: that religious belief will continue to be an important component of our shared British identity as it evolves, and that British society can and does draw strength from its diverse faith communities.

The debate about faith undoubtedly raises challenging and complex issues, but it is a national conversation we should not shy away from, and one that I am sure this timely publication will do much to further.

Introduction

by Zaki Cooper and Guy Lodge

Faith in the Nation is a unique offering from ippr, as it brings together for the first time a group of senior faith leaders in the same publication to express their views on Britishness, multiculturalism and the role of religion in the public realm. ippr sees these as vital topics to air at the current time, particularly as there are signs of a growing estrangement between the faith communities and a society increasingly characterised by individualism, cultural diversity and various kinds of fragmentation.

This publication is timely, too, given the increasing salience of a number of moral questions and policy issues that relate intimately to religious convictions and commitments. A growing sense of antagonism between some religious voices and a chorus of liberal secularists in the media and elsewhere is spilling over into political debate on such topics as faith schools and human embryology, and has arguably had a stunting impact upon our understanding of the place of faith in democratic society.

An additional rationale for this collection stems from ippr's interest and involvement in debates about the meaning and importance of national identities in our politics and public life. We sense that current debates about Britishness have tended to neglect the integral role of religious traditions and perspectives within the forging of British identity and culture. We have therefore asked all our contributors to reflect on how their own community has been received within, and has contributed to, British society.

Faith, politics and nationhood

It is often said that we now live in an age defined by identity. Many British people assert their faith as one of their primary forms of self-understanding. The 2001 Census, which for the first time asked respondents for their religion, showed that 77.2 per cent of British people identified themselves with a faith. Indeed, that Census and a

number of other surveys show that even if British people are not practising regularly, many feel as if they are affiliated to a religious
community. In the 2001 Census the vast majority of those identifying
with a faith, 71.8 per cent, did so with Christianity. But many
thousands of others ticked the box of one of our minority religions,
including Islam, Judaism, Hinduism and Sikhism.

But this is not the only reason why faith has begun to matter in
politics and public policy. The devices that were detonated by a group of
Muslim suicide bombers in London on 7 July 2005, following on from the
tragic events of 11 September 2001 in the United States, placed the issue
of religious extremism, and radical Islam in particular, firmly on the
political agenda. Intense debates have followed – about whether strong
religious identification is necessarily in tension with loyalty to Britain, and
about whether the UK's national culture and institutions need to do more
by way of granting recognition to, and space for, non-Christian cultures.
This collection presents an important opportunity to explore whether
religious affiliation aids or prevents a healthy process of cultural integration. The latter is now regarded by all sides of the political argument as
vital for a society that has seen a significant number of newly arrived
migrants land on its shores in recent years.

In fact, the presence of minority faiths in Britain, as a result of
migration patterns, is by no means new and, in the case of some faith
groups, dates back centuries. The process of inward migration has
happened fairly continually since the 1950s. Since that time Britain
has changed from a country with one dominant faith to one
comprising a large number of faith groups. Britain is a multi-faith and
multi-ethnic society. Indeed, when London successfully won its bid to
host the 2012 Olympic Games, one of its selling points was the
diversity of British society, the perfect microcosm for a global games.

The growth of religion in Britain and across the globe is in stark
contrast to most of the predictions made in the 1960s by sociologists,
the majority of whom foresaw the inexorable decline of religion. The
opposite has happened: there has been a sharp rise in religious affiliations, practices and beliefs. As the American sociologist Peter
Berger remarked in his seminal work *The Desecularisation of the
World*: 'The world today, with some exceptions ... is as furiously
religious as it ever was, and in some places more so than ever' (Berger
1999: 2).

The increasing presence and import of religion, both in terms of the identities held by many citizens and in terms of challenges facing public-policymakers, is an important backdrop to this publication. Given the tense stand-off that has developed between ardent secularists and some members of the faith communities, and the neglected potential for discussion of faith and Britishness, we thought it important to promote a more sensitive and less polemical discussion of these issues. More dialogue of this sort needs to happen between the faith communities and different branches of government, as well as with the secular public culture at large; and a deeper dialogue needs to happen between the faith communities themselves, some members of which are relatively unfamiliar with the convictions and interests of other faiths. When commissioning these authors, we were especially interested in whether the media spotlight that has recently fallen upon sharp disagreements about whether there is a role for faith in politics and the public square reflects a deepening estrangement between faith communities and a society shaped by the imperatives of commercial culture, ethno-cultural diversity and a proliferation of lifestyle choices.

Our underlying conviction is that people of faith can and should be constructively engaged by proponents of the secular public sphere, in order to tap the considerable potential that religion offers a society in which other sources of social capital are declining. More specifically, we hope that this publication will help raise the profile of an important question, considered by ippr's Michael Kenny in his concluding chapter: should public officials and authorities be encouraged to become more aware of and familiar with faith, just as many have become more aware of the presence and needs of a wider range of ethno-cultural minorities in British society?

In a context in which there is some evidence that faith communities feel more alienated and apart from the cultural mainstream, we want political progressives and liberals (even those confident in their own secularist outlook) to consider whether this is a healthy and necessary state of affairs. Not only are we in danger of overlooking the distinctive and important contribution that some faith-based activities make to the life and cohesion of communities, but we are also in danger of overlooking vital sources of civic mobilisation and social campaigning. At the same time, we should be clear and open about the real tensions that exist between the outlook and values of some religiously minded groups and individuals and the ethics of the democratic secular state, which rests upon foundational principles such as freedom of speech, the equality of all before the law, and the right to freedom from discrimination enjoyed by women, lesbians and gays. Whether these values all represent insuperable sources of offence to religious communities – as some of their supporters and opponents maintain – is an issue on which there needs to be more careful reflection.

While commentary has tended to focus exclusively upon supposed sources of fundamental disagreement between the secular public domain and religion, sources of connection and mutual benefit have been somewhat neglected. One of these, we maintain, is the history of Britain's diverse cultural heritage, and the ways in which different faith communities have become accepted presences within it. Another is the complex of experiences and stories that underpin our sense of what it is to be British. Political leaders and others have for a while now been seeking to examine the nature of British identity, and emphasising the need for a common British identity. This has been prompted by the fact that the meaning of Britishness has in recent times become a lot less certain. Whereas once the definitions revolved around the Empire and its institutions (which acted as the glue in the fabric of society), current conceptions are more fluid, pointing towards shared values and the English language. The Government, recognising this, announced in 2008 its desire to forge ahead with a British statement of values.

Communities of faith, many comprising significant numbers of people who are relatively recent arrivals in the UK, have an important perspective on the Britishness debate. They all have experience of balancing different faith and national identities. At their best, faith communities can act as agents of integration, providing the framework for a sense of belonging for ethnic and religious minorities. At their worst, they can foster feelings of separate identity that pull people away from a sense of commitment to the common good.

The distinguished group of faith leaders who have written in this publication have been invited to draw on their respective communities' perspectives, insights and experiences in reflecting on these issues. Some of them are religiously ordained, others are community representatives and figureheads. They write as leading figures in their communities, all of which are diverse and complex organisms. We have included contributions from leaders who belong to the five largest faiths in the UK: Christianity, Hinduism, Islam, Judaism and Sikhism, although that is not to diminish the contribution of some of the other faith groups in the UK, such as the Bahai's, Buddhists, Jains and Zoroastrians. Reflecting on these contributions, ippr's Michael Kenny provides some concluding insights into the potential policy implications of the issues raised.

Faith and nation – some common themes

By providing faith leaders with a platform to reflect on the relationship between faith and identity, and on the contribution their communities have made to the development of the British story, this publication raises some important issues which we hope will enrich current debate. Although their answers at times differ, it is striking to note the areas of common agreement that surface through the contributors' personal accounts. Below we summarise some of the main themes that arise in the essays that follow.

The role of religion in shaping the British national story

All the faith leaders in this collection emphasise the significant contribution that faith communities have made in helping craft the British national story. Religion, they argue, constitutes an important component of Britishness. The history of Britain is, of course, intertwined with the development of Christianity and this Christian tradition has shaped much of our language, customs and values. As Dr John Sentamu, the Archbishop of York, argues, faith and national identity in Britain have been intimately and institutionally linked for centuries. The historian Linda Colley has argued that the Protestant religion was an integral factor in forging a sense of British national identity in the eighteenth and nineteenth centuries (Colley 1992). The frustrating thing from Sentamu's perspective is that there is too little awareness of this Christian heritage in contemporary debate.

In his essay, Sentamu reasserts the case for an established Church, so that it can continue to 'serve' the nation, including Britons of other faiths and non-believers, as a whole. He senses little support for disestablishment within other faith groups, a view supported by some of the faith leaders writing here, who show how the set of arrangements that grew out of the establishment of the Church of England have quietly adapted to allow recognition for a host of other denominations and non-Christian faiths.

All the contributors express an appreciation of the capacity of British culture to allow space for different religious traditions to flourish within it. And all illustrate the impact that Britain's evolution to a multi-faith society has had on our national identity. Faith groups, for example, have transformed the built environment of Britain through the establishment of an array of institutional places of worship, such as churches, mosques and gurdwaras, the latter, for example, numbering more than 200 in Britain today. They have all contributed towards the dynamism of the UK's economy, enriched its culture, and can all boast followers who have achieved great success.

Sir Jonathan Sacks, the Chief Rabbi, reminds us of the huge contribution the Jewish community has made, for example through its role in the worlds of business, creating leading British brands like Marks and Spencer and Tesco, and culture, with writers such as Harold Pinter, and historians Simon Sharma and Martin Gilbert. Ramesh Kallidai, Secretary General of the Hindu Forum of Britain, shows how Hindus have greatly influenced British society in terms of music, arts, diet and language. Words such as 'pukka' and 'guru' have become part of everyday speech, curry is now a cornerstone of contemporary British cuisine, and thousands of Britons enjoy yoga, the ancient Hindu system of well-being. Meanwhile Dr Indarjit Singh, Director of the Network of Sikh Organisations, reflects on the enormous popularity of the England Sikh left-arm spinner, Monty Panesar.

The challenge of integration

Such examples bear witness to the significant progress that each faith group has made on the road towards cultural integration. That faith groups have made such progress on integration is no accident. All the faith leaders writing here highlight how their faiths teach the importance of civic responsibilities that go beyond the immediate community. All of them can point in their scriptures and holy books to the importance of contributing towards the state and the common good.

Nevertheless, the essays remind us that the move towards successful integration has been a struggle. Many members of faith groups have encountered intolerance and suspicion from sections of the host community. Sir Jonathan Sacks, the Chief Rabbi, reflecting on the experience of Jewish integration, writes: 'the process was not painless. Britain had prejudice as well as pride.' Cardinal Murphy-O'Connor, Archbishop of Westminster, reminds us that Catholics were a minority debarred for more than two hundred years from all positions of authority.

The challenge of integration still exists, and importantly this is not just an issue affecting the Muslim community. There is a tendency to overlook the difficult experiences that many Sikhs, Hindus and other 'world faiths' have had in securing recognition in Britain. Echoing Trevor Phillips's stark warning in 2005 that we are 'sleepwalking into segregation', some of the contributors here express concern about the worrying sign that some of our communities, including faith groups, may, to borrow the sociologist Robert Puttnam's terminology, have strong 'bonding capital' but insufficiently developed 'bridging capital'; in other words, while the internal cohesion of individual communities is high, they may not have well-developed links to the rest of society.

Migration is also a central theme to the story of integration – and it is the flows of migration that shape the actual experiences of many. Some faith groups can trace their presence in Britain back to the early modern period; and most have only become significant in numerical terms since the end of the Second World War (an exception is the Jewish community, a presence since 1656, and its major growth taking place between 1880 and 1920). The story of these minority groups, as these essays demonstrate, has a familiar pattern. It is one of arrival, followed by moves towards integration, with the communities establishing institutions and building their socio-economic strength. This is then followed by consolidation, when the communities have to struggle with challenges such as retaining their faith identity, and with prejudice and discrimination.

Cardinal Cormac Murphy-O'Connor contends that the issue of integration is made more pressing as a result of the recent migrations from Eastern Europe, Africa and South America over the past few years. The arrival into Britain of over half a million Catholics from Poland alone, he suggests, will certainly change the face of British Catholicism and Britain more widely. Indeed, many of these essays remind readers that the history of Britain is a history of immigration. The British tradition is conspicuously multi-national, multi-ethnic and multi-denomina-tional. As Daniel Defoe put it in his 1701 poem *The True Born Englishman*, 'from a mixture all kinds began, that hetr'ogeneous thing an Englishman'. The essays here show the role immigrant groups have played in enriching Britishness, and so discredit the claim made by some that immigration and diversity undermine the notion of a shared national identity.

Fostering a shared sense of Britishness and social justice

Successful integration and a loyalty to a shared British national identity can, however, be undermined by social and economic inequality. Some worrying correlations persist between socio-economic circumstances and religious background among different ethnic minorities in the UK, and pose important challenges for those committed to equality and social justice. Dilwar Hussain, Head of the Policy Research Centre at the Islamic Foundation, writes that the lack of educational achievement in sections of his community has had 'a devastating consequence on employment, community development and even self esteem' of British Muslims.

A sense of public estrangement? Religion and British national culture

These personal accounts provide compelling evidence that on the whole, most members of religious groups do not feel that they are subject to unfair or arbitrary discrimination because of their beliefs or background. This said, they also contain evidence that faith commu-nities can feel increasingly estranged from certain aspects of British culture. The reasons for this perception vary importantly between different communities. Some Muslims worry about being framed as inveterate opponents of Western values and as potential security threats. For many Hindus and Sikhs, discomfort arises from a percep-tion that their particular needs have been overlooked and a belief that they are, in the words of Ramesh Kallidai, 'something of an after-thought in public policy and interfaith dialogue'.

Despite such differences there are concerns across faith groups that the position of religion within the national public culture has become more marginal. This perception stems from a complex mixture of factors, including recoil at the rise of hedonistic and narcissistic lifestyles, the decline of traditional family structures, and the steady secularisation of the national culture that has taken place over the last few decades. A more recent cause reflects concerns that the state has come to adopt a more determinedly 'faith-blind' approach in relation to faith communities, while the development of a rights-based culture, and the extension of egalitarian principles, has come to be regarded by some religious groups as representing a worrying infraction upon the rights of religious organisations to pursue their own convictions (even despite their entitlement to exemptions from some employment regulations). A number of policy debates have flared up over same-sex couples and Catholic adoption agencies, and the Government's desire to advance scientific developments in the fields of embryology and human reproductive technologies, for instance, pitting some members of faith communities against the moral compass of the political elite.

Consequently, some of the contributors are relatively downbeat about some aspects of modern Britain: Murphy-O'Connor writes that, 'Catholics are not alone in watching with dismay as the liberal society shows signs of degenerating into the libertine society', while Sacks suggests rather alarmingly that Britain, in his view, is a much less tolerant society than it was fifty years ago. Of course there is nothing particularly new about faith leaders holding such views. At any point in history, faith leaders have struggled with aspects of modernity, and the Church has often played a role as a social critic. Such perspectives, it should be noted, are, however, balanced by the overriding message contained in these essays, which maintains that by and large Britain remains a welcoming place for people of different faiths and ethnicities.

Faith and secularism
Many of the faith leaders express concern about what they see as the emergence of a more aggressive and well-organised secularism in recent years. Murphy-O'Connor's essay is especially critical of the way he believes that some secularists have come to caricature the role of religion. He writes that: '... religious belief of any kind tends now to be treated more as a private eccentricity than as the central and formative element in British society'. He laments the rise of a fundamentalist streak within the secularist position, which, he suggests, is as intolerant and damaging as religious fundamentalism: 'the intolerance of liberal sceptics can be as repressive as the intolerance of the religious believers'. Such secularisation, he argues, should strengthen and bind

faith communities together. Singh, in his essay, contends that the concept of secularism has been transformed from a belief that in society no one religion should dominate, to one in which religious beliefs and convictions are said to offer nothing positive.

And it's the failure of some to appreciate the role played by faith-based social activism in British society that is something that frustrates the contributors. All emphasise the important role their communities play up and down the country. Sentamu talks about the 'faithful capital' produced by religious groups, citing the 23 million hours of voluntary service undertaken by members of the Church of England each year. Indeed many of Britain's leading charities were founded by Christians, including: Oxfam, Shelter, Amnesty International, Alcoholics Anonymous, Samaritans, Help the Aged, NSPCC, RSPCA, VSO, Relate, National Trust, The Children's Society, National Children's Homes, Barnado's and the modern hospice movement. Acquiring a greater understanding – through greater faith literacy – of the contribution and place of faith in British society is an issue raised throughout this collection.

Critiquing multiculturalism

A theme that arises in several of these contributions concerns a sense of unease with the multicultural framework which, some believe, has shaped how the political elite has responded to the multiplication of religions and cultures associated with inward migration over the last few decades. This has not, it is suggested, generated a durable framework for cultural integration and may have resulted in the tendency to treat cultural and faith groups as static silos, rather than dynamic communities possessing complex and changeable identities.

On the surface, such a critique of multiculturalism is perhaps surprising, especially among minority faiths. However, what is actually being criticised is the idea and experience of cultural segregation, what has been termed 'mosaic multiculturalism' (see Pearce 2007: 51). And this is what Sacks has in mind when he writes that: 'Multiculturalism leads not to integration but to segregation. It deconstructs everything that goes into making a national identity.' Other contributors argue that we need more nuanced and sinuous conceptions of multiculturalism. Dilwar Hussain warns against pursuing a 'straw man' version of multiculturalism which poses a 'singular and static policy framework', which he rightly reminds us has never really existed. He argues that, 'The social model needs to be an ever-changing one and I prefer to think of the process of integration as far more complex and fluid, through which a new narrative of the collective "we" is constantly being re-defined, giving rise to a new vision of being British (and in the context of this discussion a new vision of being Muslim naturally comes into the picture).'

A stronger sense of Britishness
Concerns about multiculturalism are, however, balanced by the view – shared by all contributors in this volume – that society needs to work together to articulate a stronger common sense of British identity. Britishness, they argue, offers an appropriate framework for the integration of ethnic and religious minorities. In contrast, they suggest, a narrowly-defined multiculturalism that promotes 'parallel lives' or a form of cultural homogeneity that favours assimilation are both anathema to a multi-national and multi-faith Britain. Britishness can act as a bridge between the legitimate claims of faith identities and a common shared set of national loyalties, which are essential for promoting community cohesion and social solidarity.

Contrary to those who argue that loyalty to a faith group compromises British identity, these contributions show that religious identities can exist alongside, and be consistent with, a common sense of Britishness. In a multi-national state, Britishness has always had to accommodate different national loyalties, and all the faith leaders represented here dismiss the notion that there is any zero-sum relationship between their religious identity and their British identity; hence the use of hyphenated identities, such as 'British-Muslim'. Faith and national identity are and must be complementary. They can be mutually reinforcing, rather than parasitic competitors.

Sacks, who provides perhaps the strongest call for strengthening national identity, says that all faith groups can unite under the roof of the British story, so long as it is honestly relayed, encompassing the failings and the successes. Sensitively told, he suggests, it is a story of hope.

Towards the secular multi-faith state
This short collection finishes with a concluding essay by ippr's Michael Kenny who reflects on how religion has re-emerged in national debate,

and how this has prompted discussion about the sort of relationship that should exist between faith and state. Kenny's essay discusses the ways in which the Manichean character of current debates about the role of faith in the public realm stunts our thinking about religion and the different roles that faith plays in the lives of people and their communities. He identifies an abiding suspicion towards, and lack of understanding of, faith within some of our public institutions, as well as the hostility of some religious communities towards the values of the liberal democratic state, as important obstacles that need to be overcome. And he makes the case for a more faith-sensitive, though not necessarily faith-sympathetic, stance to be adopted by democracies like Britain. The nuanced and engaged approach that Kenny recommends is consonant with the argument put forward by other authors in this volume for the importance of different religious traditions and communities to the heritage and culture of the UK. ippr plans to develop the ideas outlined in this concluding essay in an innovative programme of research to be conducted throughout 2009.

Finally, we would like to register our gratitude to the writers of all the articles, and hope that this publication serves as an illuminating contribution to an emerging debate.

References

Berger P (1999) *The Desecularisation of the World: Resurgent Religion and World Politics.* Washington DC: Ethics and Public Policy Center, Grand Rapids, Mich, W.B Eerdmans Pub Co.

Colley L (1992) *Britons: Forging the Nation 1707-1837* Yale University Press

Pearce N (2007) 'Not less immigration, but more integration' in Johnson N (ed.) *Britishness: towards a progressive citizenship* London: The Smith Institute

Anglicanism

by The Most Revd & Rt Hon Dr John Sentamu, Archbishop of York

The current position

> *The Government reaffirms its commitment to the position of the Church of England by law established, with the Sovereign as its Supreme Governor, and the relationship between the Church and State. The Government greatly values the role played by the Church in national life in a range of spheres.* (Secretary of State for Justice and Lord Chancellor 2007: 26, para. 62)

The above statement of relations, set out in the Government's Green paper *The Governance of Britain*, states clearly the current position of the partnership between Church and state. The Government has had cause to re-state this view more recently in response to suggestions that disestablishment is back on the agenda (*The Times*, 18 October 2008). The Ministry of Justice issued a statement in October 2008 reaffirming that: 'The Church of England is by law established and the Monarch is its Supreme Governor. The Government remains committed to this position and values the establishment of the Church of England.' (*The Times*, 22 October 2008)

The position of the Government recognises not only the historical legacy of the relationship between Church and state but also acknowledges the reality of that relationship at present, marked not so much by a position of privilege born of establishment, but rather a position of service born of duty and care.

In considering the ongoing relationship between Church and state, between faith and nation, it is worth noting the nature of the establishment before considering the challenges of pluralisation and secularisation, and concluding with thoughts on 'faithful capital' and the future of faith and nation.

What is establishment?

The establishment of the Church of England is manifest in a wide range of ways, not least through the individual daily contact of clergy who are bound by duty under establishment to serve the whole of their community, with people of all faiths and none. Some of the more visible strands of establishment include:

- The presence of a parish priest for every local community
- The right of all to be married, baptised or given a funeral through their parish church
- Helping the nation mark moments of tragedy and triumph through services, such as the recent service for police officers who have lost their lives on duty or the celebration of the bi-centenary of the abolition of the slave trade
- Helping the nation mark important royal events, such as coronations, royal weddings and funerals
- The role of the Church as a key education provider through church schools
- The laws of the Church are part of the laws of England (measures passed by the General Synod also need to be passed by Parliament), and therefore the Church's courts are part of the English legal system
- The role of the Sovereign as the Supreme Governor of the Church
- The role of the Crown in appointing bishops and some other senior clergy
- The presence of bishops in the House of Lords.

Taken together, these outward vestiges of establishment provide a basis for beginning to understand the complex nature of a relationship that has been forged over past centuries and which now finds its identity not only in these visible strands, but also in a daily engagement resulting in 'faithful capital', of which I will say more below.

The call for disestablishment

The debate on disestablishment, within and without the Church, has been alive since the seventeenth century when Puritan critics of the settlement articulated their dissatisfaction with the constitutional settlement. Critics are as often to be found within the Church as outside, with the former Bishops of both Woolwich and Birmingham both advocating the case for disestablishment over recent years (Buchanan 1994, Santer 2000). However, as Professor Owen Chadwick observed in 1970, most people were uninterested and uninformed about Church and state and as such were content to leave things as they were (Chadwick 1970). More recent critics have argued that the Church should be disestablished because it has 'ceased to be either intellectually or theologically respectable' (Gabb 2008). If respectability were the only criterion for establishment then I would take up the example of Christ and quite happily ditch respectability for the sake of the Kingdom of God.

However, there are two more substantive grounds upon which calls for disestablishment have been made: the increasing plurality of society and the growth of secularism. In my response to this I am grateful to Professor Grace Davie whose work in this area has influenced my own understanding (see Davie 2006 and Davie 2007 in particular).

Pluralisation
One of the arguments advanced by those critical of the role of the established Church is that it gives 'preference' to the Church of England above other Christian communities and other religions that have increased in numbers over recent decades, largely as a consequence of immigration, but that do not have access to 'privileges' of establishment. I think there are two reasons why such arguments are misleading and over-simplistic. The first lies in the statistical make-up of the nation and the other in a misunderstanding of how the Church of England exercises the so-called 'privilege'.

According to the last Census, published in 2001, just over three-quarters of the UK population reported having a religion. More than seven out of ten people – 72 per cent – said that their religion was Christian: some 38.4 million people. After Christianity, Islam was the most common faith with nearly 3 per cent describing themselves as Muslim (1.6 million). The next largest religious groups were Hindus (559,000), followed by Sikhs (336,000), Jews (267,000), Buddhists (152,000), and people from other religions (179,000). Together, these groups accounted for a further 3 per cent of the UK population. About 16 per cent of the UK population stated in the Census that they had no religion.

The Census religion question was a voluntary question. Nevertheless, over 92 per cent of people chose to answer it.

Such figures are the context rather than the conclusion for arguments on pluralisation. The proper acknowledgement of a society in which today different religions are visibly present with the freedom to worship and erect places of worship – on an unprecedented scale – must also be read in the context of it being a society in which the vast majority of its people describe themselves and this country as Christian, not only because of its heritage but also because of its current make-up.

One of the arguments made by pluralists against establishment is that since we now inhabit a 'multi-faith society', it is surely anachronistic to have only Church of England bishops sitting as the Lords Spiritual in the House of Lords. However, these voices rarely come from members of other faith communities who know by experience that the exercise of this aspect of establishment is done not on the Church's own behalf but for a wider constituency, of which other religions are very much a part. In practice this particular criticism is often advanced more by those using the argument of syncretism as a stalking horse for secularism.

In his *Religion in Public Life*, Roger Trigg – writing largely from a Canadian perspective – considers how the House of Lords Select Committee on Religious Offences, reporting in 2003, received a submission from the Muslim Council of Britain suggesting that changes to the law of blasphemy, which protected only the Church of England by law established, should be retained rather than abolished in attempting a 'negative equalisation' (Trigg 2007). Removing perceived privilege did not improve the situation for some; rather, it made the situation worse for all: 'from a Muslim perspective, it is better for the law to protect at least one religious denomination from blasphemy, the Anglican Church, than no religion at all' (ibid).

Writing recently in *The Times*, Melanie McDonagh put it more simply: 'leaders of minority faiths tend to be rather favourable to the Church of England position, on the ground that its bishops provide a religious take on various issues with which they usually agree' (McDonagh 2008).

Secularism
The second argument employed against establishment is that of the increased secularisation of Britain and the belief that this should lead

to a consequential decrease in the role played by the Church in society. Critics point to the decline in attendance at Church of England services and suggest that such figures mirror an attendant lack of support for the Church as a whole.

Figures for the Church of England provide a proper context for such criticism:

- 1.7 million people take part in a Church of England service each month, a level that has been maintained since the turn of the third millennium.
- Almost 3 million participate in a Church of England service on Christmas Day or Christmas Eve. 39 per cent of the population attend a church service around Christmas.
- In 2007, 43 per cent of adults attended a church or place of worship for a memorial service for someone who has died.
- 85 per cent of the population visit a church or place of worship in the course of a year, for reasons ranging from participating in worship to attending social events or simply wanting a quiet space.

The figures above, combined with the statistics from the last Census, point to a rather different picture than that painted by those who see growing secularisation as an inevitability.

The secularist argument rests on an understanding that the Church exists only to service the needs of its believers. This is where the nature of an established Church stretches beyond that attributed to it. As Archbishop William Temple is reputed to have remarked in the last century – *'the Church is the only society that exists for the benefit of its non-members.'*

This argument of 'public utility' features in the work of Professor Grace Davie, who suggests that churches, just like their parallels in health or welfare, act as a public utility, offering their services at the point of need for populations who will sooner or later require their services. Davie goes on to note that: 'the fact that these populations see no need to attend these churches on a regular basis does not mean that they are not appreciated' (Davie 2008).

This idea of 'public utility' leads to another understanding proposed by Professor Davie of 'vicarious religion': 'the notion of religion performed by an active minority but on behalf of a much larger number who (implicitly at least) not only understand, but quite clearly approve of what the minority is doing' (Davie 2007: 127).

Melanie McDonagh makes a similar point when she writes, 'But the reason, I think, why most people don't mind establishment, insofar as they think about it at all, is that it's a reassuring reminder that there is some sort of moral touchstone within the political structure. It allows non-churchgoers to identify themselves, at several removes, with Christianity in its most benign and unthreatening form' (McDonagh 2008).

Faithful capital

The idea of 'faithful capital' stands as perhaps the greatest bulwark against disestablishment in providing a reminder of what the Church is doing on a daily basis. Rooted in the parish system, it flourished from a concern for people of all faiths and none and is fed by a desire to bring about the common good, in all areas of our nation.[1]

More than twenty years ago a report from the Church of England, *Faith in the City* (Archbishop of Canterbury's Advisory Group on Urban Priority Areas 1985), ignited a wide-ranging political debate on urban life in 1980s Britain. The conclusion of the report left little doubt of the state in which many urban dwellers found themselves: '... a growing number of people are excluded by poverty or powerlessness from sharing in the common life of our nation. A substantial minority – perhaps as many as one person in every four or five across the nation – are forced to live on the margins of poverty or below the threshold of an acceptable standard of living' (ibid: 359).

The report spoke of *fabric decay, economic decline,* and *social disintegration* and one of the many outcomes it prompted was the establishment of the Church Urban Fund which continues to invest £3 million annually in vital grassroots projects in the poorest urban communities on behalf of the Church of England as a whole. (Since its creation the Fund has made grants of over £64 million to communities.)

---

1. Although this section concentrates on the work of the Church in urban areas, the Church has an equally distinguished record of service in rural areas through bodies such as the Arthur Rank Centre and the work of those Church of England dioceses that serve areas that are predominantly rural in their makeup.

Twenty years after the publication of *Faith in the City*, the Church embarked on a new inquiry into urban life in light of the changed world in British cities. The result was a new report, *Faithful Cities: A call for celebration, vision and justice*, which argues that there is more to life than economic and cultural regeneration, and that the wellbeing and renewal of our cities must be grounded in a vision of justice and human dignity (The Commission on Urban Life and Faith 2006). What makes a good city is its generous people who create safe neighbourhoods through their active volunteering.

One of the findings of *Faith in the City* was that at their best, churches – alongside those of other faiths – offer a particular gift to communities, something the report calls 'faithful capital'. This is a development of the idea of 'social capital', an idea used by social theorists to express the way in which people are enriched not only by what they have or what they can do but by their web of social relationships and their participation in civic life. The report identified the powerful influence of 'faithful capital' in the long term, not least through the presence and engagement of people of faith in our most deprived urban areas. No doubt because of its parish system, the Church of England, in particular, is home to buildings and networks of people dedicated to the long-term service of the local urban neighbourhood. The report found that not only are faith communities in our cities physically present, they are actively, dutifully and sometimes passionately, engaged in caring and campaigning for those who need care most – sometimes people whom the wider 'society' has forgotten.

With regard to relations between state and nation, this social and 'faithful capital' can be seen as both a valuable resource and a source of discomfort. On the one hand, they offer paths to the grails of 'community cohesion' and urban 'regeneration'. On the other, the distinct and conflicting language of faith, the values that challenge rather than support government policy, and working styles that fail to mesh with time-limited, benchmark-driven, outcome-required government schemes can pose a huge challenge.

Since the publication of *Faithful Cities*, an independent report has been published, by the Von Hügel Institute, which outlines the work undertaken by the Church of England in its welfare provision for the nation (Davis *et al* 2008). One of the report's conclusions was that the Government is fundamentally underestimating the number of

Christian charities, the work of such charities and consequently their social, economic and civic impact and potential. Through their own research into the social, economic and civic impact of churches, the authors highlighted the important roles of bishops, dioceses and cathedrals. They also note that they found congregations, clergy and volunteers running post offices and cafes, doctors' surgeries and asylum rights centres, homeless outreach and bereavement counselling, job creation and economic regeneration programmes, environmental initiatives and youth clubs, peace networks and third-world solidarity groups.

The 'faithful capital' identified by the *Faithful Cities* report remains strong and vital in its service of entire communities throughout our nation. The findings of the Von Hügel Report underscore that fact.

Any belief that the established relationship between Church and state is defined solely by reference to constitutional settlements, the presence of Bishops in the Lords or through national engagement needs to be re-considered in light of the 'faithful capital' being employed each day by the Church in communities throughout the nation.

In speaking of establishment we must also have due regard to the existence of the parish system as the place where establishment is most real and accessible. That is where it happens: a place of worship and service to the nation.

Conclusions

At a time when a creeping social Darwinism is on the rise, where life is measured in terms of its 'quality' or 'usefulness', the Church remains the last bastion of defence for those who would find themselves close to jettison by society. The doors of the Church are never shut in that they embrace an understanding of humanity and the individual where all life is God-given and God-breathed. There is no measure or qualification of 'usefulness' but only the very act of being alive. In this sense the Church reasserts those principles at the very heart of equality and human rights: the infinite worth of every human being.

Hence the Church becomes a place not only for the most vulnerable but also for their most vocal defenders; a tent pitched in the middle of the public square where all are invited because all are worthy. It is a place where divine action and human activity overlap in the person of Jesus Christ, with His altar at the centre of the tent pitched among us. Not simply a place of refuge, but rather a place of hospitality for the marginalised, welcoming those who find themselves, by accident or design, at risk of exclusion from any sense of belonging or without a stake in our stakeholding society.

The Church also remains the place, overwhelmingly, where people gather to grieve for those shared public events that require a retreat from the daily business of activity to somewhere more reflective, where a grieving community exists. Whether it be the public tragedies of 11 September 2001, 7 July 2005, the death of Diana, Princess of Wales, or the murders of Holly Wells and Jessica Chapman, the public outpouring of grief and shock found their voice and physical presence in the churches of their communities. Perhaps more importantly, every day the Church provides the community for those who are bereaved, to grieve alongside, to offer thanksgiving *in memoria* and to offer care.

There is little doubt in my mind that a place exists for an established Church serving our nation. From church schools to funerals, from inter-faith work to state occasions, from speaking out for the marginalised to ministering to the sick, the Church plays a vital daily role in the operation of our nation.

The Church of England, itself part of the world-wide Church, has given birth to churches in 166 countries. I myself benefited from the educational work of English, Scottish and Welsh missionaries in my country of birth, Uganda. Now, as a Christian and Archbishop in England, I simply remind the English of what they first taught me. I am amazed that there is so little consciousness of this rich heritage. We need to become better acquainted with this legacy, be grateful for it, rediscover its dynamic and build upon it. The spiritual wealth and 'faithful capital' that made this country great is to be shared not only with present and future generations in the UK, but as a free gift from God to the whole of humanity.

A nation with a clear, shared view of itself, of its basic values and beliefs, and the behaviour that those within society can expect from each other, will be better prepared to face up to the challenges of the modern world, be they the impacts of globalisation, different working patterns, an increasingly mobile population, or the challenges of climate change, not forgetting the turbulence in the money markets.

Who would have ever thought that money as a means of exchanging goods would become the leading brand of goods with a market of its own!

For the Church in England must once again be a beacon by which the people of England can orientate themselves in an unknown ocean by offering them the Good News of God in Christ in practical and relevant ways to their daily lives. The Church in England must rediscover the self-confidence and self-esteem that united and energised the English people those many centuries ago when the disparate fighting groups embraced the message and invitation of God's love in Jesus Christ.

The current challenge for the Church of England, as I believe it is also for other denominations, is to ensure that it is proclaiming the Gospel afresh in a way that is comprehensible and relevant to people today: inviting them to participate in the death and resurrection of Jesus Christ.

And I am hopeful. There are many signs that the Church is beginning to find again that renewal which lies at the heart of our resurrection faith. I see it in the 23 million hours of voluntary service that members of the Church of England provide to their communities each year. I see it in the work that Anglicans along with Christians of other denominations and those of other religions are doing to campaign and provide for asylum seekers. I see it in the work of Church Academies seeking to transform areas of need and deprivation into places of learning, service and hope. In responding to the needs of these most vulnerable people the Church is indeed fulfilling the Biblical imperatives to stand up for the poor and defenceless and to care for the stranger in its midst.

The Church finds its energy, vision and purpose in the life, death and resurrection of Jesus Christ. This earth-shattering event gave the Church its momentum. The physicality of Jesus's resurrected body is the prototype and promise of new creation. It opens the way for us to discern and obey God's loving purpose for planet earth and for every nation and person on it. There is no place for spectators, for we are all invited to be active collaborators with our Creator.

As Archbishop William Temple wrote at the conclusion of his book *Christianity and the Social Order*: 'I should give a false impression of my own convictions if I did not here add that there is no hope of establishing a more Christian social order except through the labour and sacrifice of those in whom the spirit of Christ is active, and that the first necessity for progress is more and better Christians taking full responsibility as citizens for the political, social and economic system under which they and their fellows live' (Temple 1942: 98).

References

Archbishop of Canterbury's Advisory Group on Urban Priority Areas (ACUPA) (1985) *Faith in the City: A Call for Action by Church and Nation* London: Church House Publishing

Buchanan C (1994) *Cut the Connection: Disestablishment and the Church of England* London: Darton, Longman & Todd Ltd

Chadwick O (1970) *Church and State: Report of the Archbishop's Commission* London: Church Information Office

Commission on Urban Life and Faith, The (2006) *Faithful Cities: A call for celebration, vision and justice,* London: Methodist Publishing House and Church House Publishing

Davie G (2006) 'Vicarious religion: A methodological challenge', in Ammerman N (ed) *Everyday Religion: Observing Modern Religious Lives,* New York: Oxford University Press

Davie G (2007) *The Sociology of Religion,* London: Sage

Davie G (2008) 'Debate' in Wells S and Coakley S (eds.) *Praying for England: Priestly Presence in Contemporary Culture,* London: Continuum

Davis F, Paulhus E and Bradstock A (2008) *Moral, But No Compass – Government, Church, and the Future of Welfare* Cambridge/Chelmsford: Von Hügel Institute/Matthew James Publishing

Gabb S (2008) 'Should the Church be disestablished? Yes, says Dr Sean Gabb' *The Times,* 24 October

McDonagh M (2008) 'Minister, leave the Church of England alone' *The Times,* 23 October

Santer M (2000) Presidential Address to Diocesan Synod

Secretary of State for Justice and Lord Chancellor (2007) *The Governance of Britain,* CM 7170, July, London: HMSO

Temple W (1942) *Christianity and the Social Order* London: Shepheard-Walwyn

Trigg R (2007) *Religion in Public Life* Oxford: Oxford University Press

Catholicism

by Cardinal Cormac Murphy-O'Connor, Archbishop of Westminster

The history of Catholicism in Britain goes back to the beginnings of the English state and beyond. It was interrupted in the 16th century by the Reformation, which had the effect of dividing Christianity in these islands into different branches. Catholicism remained one of them; but the Church of England, 'Catholic and reformed', was seen by the majority of the British people as the continuation of the pre-Reformation English church. With the papal Bull *Regnans in Excelsis* excommunicating Queen Elizabeth I, followed by the Gunpowder Plot (condemned by the Pope, incidentally), Catholics became the most suspect of all the dissenting bodies.

From a Catholic perspective, the Catholic Church here, despite having become a small and unpopular minority, was not just the lineal descendant of the pre-Reformation English church, but identical with it; and the assumption of that role by the Church of England was seen as a usurpation. Both churches cherished the memory of their mutual injuries, and Catholics, as a minority debarred for more than two hundred years from all positions of authority or influence in the state, developed a strong, distinctive and to some degree exclusive *esprit de corps*.

Following the Catholic Emancipation Act of 1829, Catholics gradually re-entered British national life. Upper and middle class Catholics tended to compensate for the suspicion with which they were still regarded by an intensified loyalty to Britain and to the Crown. Meanwhile the huge nineteenth century flood of immigrants from Ireland had created a strong Catholic working class whose political sympathies were first with the Irish Home Rule Party and later with the Labour Party.

The Oxford Movement of the 1830s strengthened the Catholic dimension of the Church of England, while bringing into the Catholic Church itself an infusion of highly educated converts, among them Newman and Manning, whose intellectual formation and outlook were totally different, both from the 'old Catholics' on the one hand and from the Irish immigrants on the other. Relations between Catholics and Anglicans, however, were still poisoned by suspicion and hostility, so that an eminent Anglican could famously dismiss the Catholic Church in England as 'the Italian mission to the Irish'.

Although relations between the churches steadily improved in the first part of the twentieth century as more and more Catholics entered the professions and played an increasing part in public life, Anglicanism and Catholicism were still generally spoken of as distinct 'religions' and to be an 'RC' carried overtones of oddity and otherness. 'But many of my best friends are Jews' was a syndrome which applied also (behind their backs) to Catholics. Catholics for their part were forbidden to take part in Anglican or other non-Catholic services of any kind and 'mixed marriages' between Catholics and non-Catholics were officially discouraged. This was still the climate in which those of us now in our seventies grew up; and it was not until the 1950s that a dramatic change for the better gathered momentum, greatly acceler-ated by the Second Vatican Council of the 1960s and its aftermath.

Another important factor bringing the churches together has undoubtedly been the progressive secularisation of the cultural envi-ronment and the accompanying decline in religious practice, so that religious belief of any kind tends now to be treated more as a private eccentricity than as the central and formative element in British society that it is. And although the tone of public discussion is sceptical or dismissive rather than anti-religious, atheism has become more vocal and aggressive. This unfriendly climate for people of all religious faiths has led to the recognition that what we have in common as Christian believers is infinitely more important than what divides us – a consideration that now applies not only to the Christian Churches, but in different degrees to relations between all three monotheistic faiths, Christianity, Judaism and Islam. It is significant that one of the most articulate and respected defenders of religious values in Britain today is the Chief Rabbi.

The privatisation of religious belief and the increasingly multiracial character of what was previously a more or less homogeneous society has also had the effect of diminishing the social 'oddness' of belonging to any particular denomination or faith. Over the past 40 years social prejudice against Catholics has largely disappeared and Catholics have been fully assimilated into the mainstream of British life. Intellectual and cultural acceptance, however, is another matter; and there is a widely perceived conflict between religious belief (and the Catholic Church in particular) on the one hand and the prevailing notion of what it means to be a 'liberal' and tolerant society on the other.

Leaving aside the polemical views of Professor Dawkins and his fellow atheists on the essential irrationality of all religious belief, there is a current dislike of absolutes in any area of human activity, including morality (though this does not apparently preclude an absolute ban on anything that can be interpreted as racial, sexual or gender discrimination). In part, this dislike stems from an entirely understandable revulsion for totalitarianism; and there is no denying that too absolutist an approach to ethical problems leads to intolerance. But as the ongoing debate about faith schools has demonstrated, the intolerance of liberal sceptics can be as repressive as the intolerance of religious believers.

What should be the limits of tolerance in a liberal society is a key question in the wider current debate about 'multiculturalism'. Because of the Catholic experience of what it means to be a credal minority, British Catholics are likely to sympathise with those ethnic and religious groups who want to retain their cultural and religious distinctiveness in a British environment.

The issue of integration is made more pressing as a result of the migrations from Eastern Europe, Africa and South America over the past few years. This has been most vividly demonstrated by the arrival into Britain of over half a million Catholics from Poland and they alone will certainly change the face of British Catholicism. The growth of ethnic chaplaincies, especially in London, offers a support that is familiar but as with previous migrations, integration into existing communities is already taking place through school and work. Young, socially conservative and many from countries that are predominantly Catholic, their integration into a liberal, tolerant society of many faiths and none will be helped by the experiences of British Catholics.

Despite the often quoted example of Northern Ireland, diversity of belief and practice is not necessarily divisive in a way that endangers social cohesion or the public good. Of course immigrant groups have an obligation to understand, respect and adjust to the ethos of the society they are opting to join. Our society has a corresponding obligation to encourage and help them to do so. But we should beware of those liberals who, as Roger Scruton has remarked, can tolerate any belief whatsoever, only so long as it is not seriously held.[2]

For Catholics, the conflict with liberal opinion focuses at the present time on two issues on which the Catholic position is characterised as intolerant and (even worse!) 'reactionary': the absolute value of every human life; and the central importance of the family and the institution of marriage as fundamental pillars of a rightly ordered society. Many other Christians, as well as Jews and Muslims, broadly share the Catholic Church's position on these issues, but I think it is fair to say that the Catholic Church bears the brunt of 'liberal' hostility on both fronts.

What does all this tell us about the relationship between Catholicism and British identity? Clearly, there are serious tensions – as there should be – between Christian belief and the assumptions and practices of a secular state; and Catholics are not alone in watching with dismay as the liberal society shows signs of degenerating into the libertine society. While a questioning of authority is healthy in holding authority to account, this questioning can, at its most extreme, become rejection. Undermining the pillars of British society (Parliament, monarchy, Church) risks dismantling not only the institutions but also the values that have underpinned British identity.

One area of specific concern for the Catholic Church is marriage and family life. The British enthusiasm for debate and tolerance of alternative views has led to an acceptance of diversity and pluralism. This is welcome, but if an acceptance of diversity and pluralism becomes an end in itself there is a grave risk that long-accepted cultural norms, such as marriage and family, are undermined to the detriment of society as a whole. The vocal minority who argue that religion has no role in modern British society portray Catholic teaching on the family as prejudiced and intolerant to those pursuing alternatives. Catholic teaching is clear that all unjust discrimination is wrong, but this teaching cannot accept the relativistic acceptance that all approaches are equivalent.

---

2. 'In my experience the most intolerant people are liberals: people who can tolerate any belief whatsoever, provided it is not seriously held, and who therefore demonise everyone who really disagrees with them.' Review in *The Times*, 29 April 1999

British society champions tolerance and freedom, but that freedom is dependent on responsibility. A simplistic belief that right or wrong is an individualistic construct denies our responsibilities to neighbour and wider society. These responsibilities are defined through negotiation and the Catholic Church is not seeking a privileged position in putting forward its position (be it on the value of Catholic schools to a cohesive society, a vocational approach to healthcare or the recent issue of Catholic adoption agencies, which seek to provide a vital public service, guided by Catholic teaching); it merely asks that it is not excluded from the public square precisely because it is the Catholic Church. The need for an open, tolerant and vibrant public square is more essential than ever as the competing rights of the individual, backed by a Human Rights Act, increasingly come into conflict with the rights of religious groups to act according to their conscience and beliefs.

But as citizens of the United Kingdom we are fortunate to live in a country where the Christian ethos is still, despite the best efforts of secularists, pervasive. The UK, said a House of Lords Select Committee in 2003, 'is not a secular state...the constitution of the United Kingdom is rooted in faith – specifically the Christian faith, exemplified by the established status of the Church of England'.

At the same time – for all the distortions and inadequacies of the media – there is an equally pervasive tradition of genuine tolerance and freedom of debate; indeed the Glorious Revolution of 1688 was made in the name of rights in general and of religious freedom in particular. While Catholics and Jews were initially excluded, this did eventually lead to the Catholic Emancipation Act and the integration of Catholics back into the life of the nation.

The task of British Catholics – together with our fellow Christians and all believers of goodwill – is not to opt out of the debate or to fall back on anathemas, but to work by reasoned argument, and above all by the example of our own lives, to strengthen the many features of British society that we believe to be good and to correct those that we believe to be wrong.

Judaism

by Sir Jonathan Sacks, Chief Rabbi

The history of modern British Jewry goes back to 1656 when the government of the day gave permission to Jews to worship openly as Jews. It took another two centuries for them to achieve civic equality. Not until 1858, for example, were Jews permitted to become members of Parliament. Yet they saw Britain as a pioneer of tolerance and were intensely loyal to the country.

They placed the highest possible value on integration, especially during the years of mass immigration between the 1880s and 1914. In 1881 the *Jewish Chronicle* wrote about the newly arrived East European Jews: 'If they intend to remain in England, if they wish to become members of our community, we have a right to demand that they will show signs of an earnest wish for a complete amalgamation with the aims and feelings of their hosts.'

Institutions like the Jews' Free School trained pupils to be model Englishmen and women. Louis Abrahams, head teacher of JFS from 1898 until 1900, urged parents to reinforce the message of the school:

Strengthen the efforts of the teachers to wipe away all evidence of foreign birth and foreign proclivities, so that your children shall be so identified with everything that is English, in thought and deed, that no shadow of anti-Semitism might exist, that your boys and girls may grow up devoted to the flag which they are learning within these walls to love and honour, that they may take a worthy part in the growth of this great Empire, whose shelter and protection I hope will never be denied them.

Such efforts were successful. By 1895 a reporter from the *Daily Graphic* who had visited the school reported: 'When they leave, they all speak English with a regard for grammar and a purity of accent far above the average of the neighbourhood.' Jews developed a love of Britain that was deep and genuine.

In the integration of minorities, role models are essential. In the case of Victorian Jewry, a key figure was Sir Moses Montefiore, an observant Jew, President of the Board of Deputies of British Jews, well known to the general public, Sheriff of the City of London and a close personal friend of Queen Victoria.

On his ninety-ninth, and again on his hundredth birthday, *The Times* published leaders in his honour. The latter, on 24 October 1884, is particularly fascinating. It speaks of Montefiore's philanthropy to Christians and Jews alike. It pays tribute to the synthesis he had created between the two identities: 'He has been the victorious defender of persecuted Jews because he was the perfect English gentleman.' In his own person he had 'solved once for all the problem of the competence of the most faithful of Jews to be not the less a complete Englishman.' The article ended with a stern admonition to the rest of the Jewish community to follow his example: 'the determination to show, by his life, that fervent Judaism and patriotic citizenship are absolutely consistent with one another'.

The contrast between Britain then and now is marked. In those days Britain knew who and what it was. It had an identity, a shared moral code, and most importantly, pride. It had the self-confidence without which no society can be at peace with itself. It granted minorities freedom to practise their religion, but it expected them, culturally and in other ways, to become part of British society. Both sides gained. Britain retained its character. Minorities learned to adjust, adapt and belong.

The process was not painless. Britain had prejudice as well as pride. In 1887 a letter writer to *The Times* complained of 'foreign paupers replacing English workers and driving to despair men, women and children of our blood.' The *East London Advertiser* identified the culprits: 'The swarms of foreign Jews who have invaded the East End labour market are chiefly responsible ...' In 1903 the MP for Stepney, Major Evans Gordon, said at a constituency meeting, 'There is hardly an Englishman in this room who does not live under the constant danger of being driven from his home, pushed out into the streets, not by the natural increase of our own population, but by the off-scum of Europe.'

The off-scum eventually integrated, among them creators of businesses including Marks and Spencer, Tesco and Shell Petroleum, writers such as Harold Pinter and Peter Schaffer, historians like Simon

Schama and Martin Gilbert, theatre and film producers, politicians, academics, soldiers, judges, boxers, poets, philosophers, Nobel Prize winners and two of the last four Lord Chief Justices. There is a story of hope here. The same abuse directed at Jews a hundred years ago has been turned successively on other immigrant populations. Yet each has gone on to enrich our culture.

The story of British Jewry is proof, if proof be needed, of how mistaken the policy of multiculturalism is – and I say this as one who has written a book called *The Dignity of Difference*. Multiculturalism leads not to integration but to segregation. It deconstructs everything that goes into the making of a national identity: a shared culture, a canon of texts everyone is expected to know, a collective history and memory, a code of conduct and civility, and a sense of loyalty to the nation and its institutions. No society can long survive without these things.

Jews, like other minorities, integrated because there was something to integrate into. They did so because they respected British values: otherwise they would not have come here. Today all three words – 'respect', 'British' and 'values' – have become thoroughly opaque. Values have become relativised, 'British' hard to define, almost devoid of content, and 'respect' something more often invoked than practised. Britain in the strictest sense of the word has become de-moralised: it has lost a common code. It is losing a sense of the common good.

When societies become demoralised, they become politicised. Institutions that were once expressions of shared belonging – univer-sities, professional bodies, houses of worship, places where you left your politics outside – have been turned, one after another, into pressure groups, complete with boycotts, disinvestment campaigns and lobbying activities, usually on matters of foreign policy. Spaces that once united citizens regardless of their political affiliations, now divide them. This erodes civil society.

Multiculturalism, therefore, designed to make minorities feel more at home, has had the opposite effect. Britain is a less tolerant society today than it was fifty years ago when I was at school. The schools I went to were Christian, yet never once did I experience anti-Semitism. Many of our children and grandchildren do experience it. Our post-modern culture with its moral relativism and its emphasis on rights

rather than responsibilities has, by the law of unintended conse-
quences, made things worse, not better.

The time has come to strengthen our identity as a nation. We need
to teach the British story – and it is an unusual story. The Britain that
admitted Jews in 1656 was the same one that had expelled them in
1290. There are aspects of the past – Britain's class divisions, the
exploitation of the poor, the imperial legacy – that are less than
perfect. Britain's greatness lay in the fact that it was willing to
confront its failings and redress them. It was a nation willing to learn,
change, make sacrifices in the service of ideals, and grow. Sensitively
told, it is a story of hope.

How can we expect minorities to feel pride in being British if the
majority does not? How can we ask them to respect British institutions
if they are ruthlessly pilloried in the media? How can we expect
Hindus, Sikhs, Muslims and others to be loyal to the British way of life
if there is no longer any consensus on what that way of life actually
is? One aspect of the British story is of how an island nation became
home to successive groups of immigrants, each of which added to its
culture and creative energies. It is a story that now embraces us all.

Politicians rightly find it hard to speak about these issues. Just as
an earlier age (substantively if not constitutionally) separated Church
and state, so ours separates morality and state... which brings us back
to the question of the role of religion in Britain today.

Religion is an agent of social change, the most powerful there is.
Almost every other institution today offers us what we want. Religion
teaches us what to want. It is the last refuge of what philosophers call
second-order evaluation. It tells us that there is something beyond
autonomy, rights and the satisfaction of desire. It speaks unashamedly
of duty, compassion, responsibility, loyalty, obligation, the sanctity of
life, the sacred bond of marriage, and the covenant of human solidarity. It tells us that our worth is not measured by how much we earn
or what we buy, but by the good we do and the love we create.

Much therefore depends on how religion develops in Britain in the
future. Will religious groups turn inward to protect their own values or
will they join hands to help heal divided communities and a fractured
society? The time has come for the religious groups in Britain to join
in creating a *covenant of the common good*, a commitment to work
together to promote active citizenship and a sense of shared

belonging. I would like to see this spread outward to embrace schools, charities and local associations.

The best advice ever given to religious minorities was that of the prophet Jeremiah twenty-six centuries ago, when he told the Jews who had been exiled to Babylon: 'Seek the welfare of the city to which you have been carried and pray to God on its behalf, for if it prospers, you too will prosper.' A diverse society need not be a divided society if we see it as the home we build together – and if we bring our differences as contributions to the common good.

Islam

by Dilwar Hussain, Policy Research Centre, Islamic Foundation

Islam and the British Isles have had centuries of interaction. The mention, in Arabic, of the Muslim declaration of faith on coins minted by King Offa (d. 796) is a cryptic example of this. Despite this early interaction it was probably in the eighteenth century that the first Muslims began to make Britain their home. As they were mainly sailors, most of the early communities were formed in areas of the major port cities. Two significant communities also sprang up in Woking and Liverpool in the late nineteenth century, with a number of converts and trainee civil servants from the Indian subcontinent playing an important role in these cities. These communities were quite small and localised and it was much later, after the Second World War, that more significant numbers of Muslims migrated and settled in the UK, mostly from the rural areas of Pakistan and Bangladesh. Over the years, these communities have been joined by Muslims originating from Africa, Arab countries, Europe and the Far East, as well as a small number of converts from the UK, to form an ethnically diverse and culturally vibrant community of communities.

This cultural vibrancy has meant that over the last fifty years Muslims have become quite visible, whether through the growth of Indian restaurants (mostly British-Bangladeshi owned), clothing and grocery outlets selling exotic merchandise, buildings with ornate eastern architecture, or the infamous dress of some Muslim women. And then, of course, there is terrorism. But long before the security challenge, other issues were creating debate, some of the major topics being education, discrimination, identity, family values, leadership and representation.

Despite the strong emphasis on learning in Muslim culture, socio-economic circumstances have often meant that significant sections of the Muslim community were among the weakest performers in educational terms. Arguably, this lack of achievement has had a devastating consequence on employment, community development and even self esteem. Many of the first generation of Muslims to live in the UK faced racist abuse, but more recently that xenophobia seems to have become more specific, focusing on religion as a marker in addition to the different skin colour of most Muslims. This 'Islamophobia' has now been written about extensively, and in a 1997 report published by the Runnymede Trust, was deemed to be a serious issue for British society.

For many Muslims of the second and third generation, one of the major issues of discussion has been identity. This evolving debate has seen new twists and turns in the post 9/11 and 7/7 era. For the vast majority the story has always been of people who saw great opportunities in the UK, people who were born, or at least brought up, here with a sense of pride and belonging – right down to the neighbourhood level – often displayed in the local accents, cultures and customs adopted by Muslims across the country. This process of adoption and adaptation has quite naturally created a gradually developing sense of hyphenated identities such as 'British-Pakistani-Muslim', or later just 'British-Muslim'. It seems that the crucial 'problem' lies in how Muslims can become entirely comfortable being British and at the same time maintain strong ties with their faith. Can this apparently dual sense of loyalty be harmonised?

Increasingly, people have argued that in fact the problem implicit in the above questions is down to their framing. People have always juggled multiple identities. The tensions in loyalty, whether the pulls are towards individual interest, family, ideology or belief, nation or the world, have always involved a negotiated exercise of judgement in which a sharp sense of justice is a vital yardstick. It is for this reason that the Qur'an instructs, 'be just, even if it is against yourself, your parents or kin'. Such a discourse identifies that being loyal to one's faith is ultimately about being a good person – in not only a private context, but also in a public setting: that is, being a good citizen, working for justice, and to promote the common good.

But the religious label accorded to Muslim citizens does now appear to have some problematic dimensions. Increasingly, Muslim identity is viewed as reified and exaggerated. A criminal is now a 'Muslim thief', the local GP is a 'Muslim doctor', and so on. The trouble with this is that Muslims cannot be seen simply as human beings: they have to be perceived mainly through a religious prism. Eventually, I hope, the label can just be 'British' (or even 'English' for those of us in England).

In saying this I am not suggesting that Muslims disappear into a secular void, rather that Islam is no longer an exotic preoccupation: it becomes banal and ordinary, normal and normalised. We would not usually feel the need to call Gordon Brown a 'Christian Prime Minister', even though Christianity is evidently important to him. It is all about how we choose to define people publicly, and giving them a one-dimensional description, however important, undervalues the complexity of that person.

In some cases loyalties have conflicted dangerously, and much has been written on the menace of violent extremism. However small the number of those radicalised in this way, the nature of the threat means that it must be taken seriously.

Much could be said about Britain's foreign policy mistakes in stoking injustice, leading to anger and frustration. But to blame only such foreign affairs for terrorism is not nearly enough. Muslims did not challenge strongly enough the preachers of hate and the peddlers of simplistic, yet nihilistic, solutions that were able to tap into that anger and frustration. Nor did they create adequate religious institutions or leadership that could connect with young people and educate them in an idiom they would understand, something that could have protected them when challenged by extremists' discourse. If we can learn such lessons and move on, perhaps things can be different.

No doubt, a religious identity also raises other questions – should faith not be a private affair? How can we manage the public realm if people overtly bring up contesting ideas that could fragment national solidarity? Is there not an urgent need for integration into a national narrative? Do we not need to go beyond the errors of multiculturalism, which emphasised difference?

Of course, having an overarching national identity and bringing one's own ideas and values to the table are not mutually exclusive. The word 'integration' often receives a mixed response, usually because it is not defined clearly and because the assumptions behind it are not always disclosed openly. Whenever I use this word, it is to place it somewhere between (and distinct from) social or cultural segregation and total assimilation. Assimilation would seem to involve one entity dissolving into something else (as salt dissolves into water and ceases to be salt).

Sometimes 'integration' seems to be used to mean assimilation, a differential usage that can be seen especially in pan-European discussions. At times the word is used to imply two distinct, essentialised entities coming together and one becoming part of the other, the onus being on one to integrate into the other.

As for multiculturalism, I think the problem has been in viewing it as a singular and static policy framework, when in fact, it has never been thus. Up and down the country over the last 30 years policies have often changed as needs have evolved. We can, of course, argue that in places policies need to change even more, and that mistakes have been made. Many of us felt in the 1980s that the emphasis on different languages, cultures and ethnic needs were contributing to barriers between groups in society. But the overall thrust, and value, of multiculturalism was to develop a sense of respect for difference, during a very different climate from today's, at a time when race relations were far more tense.

The model needs to be ever-changing and I prefer to think of the process of integration as far more complex and fluid, through which we can constantly redefine a new narrative of the collective 'we', and give rise to new visions of being British (and in the context of this discussion a new vision of being Muslim naturally comes into the picture).

Sometimes an assumption in the discourse is that integration will lead to less apparent, less visible minorities, or perhaps to less troublesome ones. This may be an unrealistic assumption to make as integration is likely to increase the assertiveness of groups – as a natural by-product of an increased sense of ownership of the nation. Whereas immigrant grandparents would pass by a racist incident on the streets with their heads down, youngsters who feel a greater sense of ownership of the space around them and that they can demand equal treatment may not be as passive.

But if channelled properly and maturely, an aggressive, even radical, form of citizenship is no bad thing for democracy. Broad-based community-organising groups, such as the Citizen Organising Foundation's network, show very successfully how passion can be harnessed into politics, and how this can actually unite communities rather than divide them, when combined with pragmatism and a strong sense of the local common good. At a time when we are worried about participation and voter attendance, it is vital to harness people's energies rather than to try to pacify them. Furthermore, a real stake in power and the experience of effecting change is vital to the integration process.

One very useful way of thinking about integration was developed by the Commission for Racial Equality. Integration was seen to have three pillars: equality, participation and interaction. This encompasses the need for the playing field to be levelled and 'glass ceilings', as barriers to achievement and ambition, removed; a commitment to participating in the system and engaging as citizens; and the need for spaces in which different people can interact. Clearly, such a vision for integration removes the onus from any single entity or group and speaks more about the climate necessary for people to come together.

Bearing the above in mind, I will now propose some priorities that I feel may enhance the relationship between faith and nation (vis-à-vis the Muslim presence):

For Muslim communities:

1. A stronger and more rooted sense of British identity, of ownership of the local space and living among the people as 'our people'.

2. Evolution of a new contextual theology of Islam that is rooted in Muslim sources and tradition, but is read and expressed to deal with the challenges of the new contexts that Muslims face. Among these challenges a key issue is to resolve the inequalities in gender relations found in some misogynistic Muslim cultures. Furthermore, for a religion that developed much of its worldview and theology in a context of being the majority there is a need now to develop ideas around diasporic and minority status, particularly in the context of living in a plural, secular space. Can Islam develop a British flavour? I would ague that it can and must.

3. Engagement and participation, but on a human and plural basis, not purely for parochial ends. Can Muslims defend the rights of others to be treated equally even in cases where the values of the 'other' may be at odds with 'our' values? Evidently, we cannot stand on a liberal pedestal to claim equal treatment, and then aim

to deny that very right to others. Living up to such a consistent moral framework requires some considerable soul-searching about the core values of Islam, and its priorities.

4. Education, for the young all the way to training of Imams and leaders. In the context of nurturing Imams, this is, crucially, about the curriculum and the methods of education, not only the language or medium of communication. Are Imams able to equip people in dealing with contemporary challenges? Do they develop a more plural outlook? Or do they perpetuate an isolationist mindset?

5. Realisation that the state cannot solve everything. State power and state patronage have their roles, but they also have important limitations. The state can facilitate, but Muslims need to develop their position in civil society by investing in it, and working in partnership with others to build horizontal alliances. Aspects of Muslim discourse coming out of a post-colonial, post-Caliphate 20th century have arguably placed far too much emphasis on state, and not enough on society.

For the nation:

1. Greater recognition of Muslims and their contribution to the collective European heritage, especially in areas such as mathematics, science and philosophy. Unless we are able to move beyond the notion of Muslims being a cultural and intellectual 'other', very little progress can be made.

2. Greater equality and a level playing field, particularly focusing on socio-economic issues, opportunities and life chances.

3. A more open civic space that respects difference, where trust is built, so that there is greater interaction and room for honest conversations between communities and groups. This in turn will help to build long-term cohesion across communities.

4. Public education on religion (and Islam in the context of this

essay) in order to raise literacy on some of the issues that are being debated – ironically, the solution (as many have now recognised) is more religion, not less. This will help to raise the level of debate on issues such as tackling violent extremism and also give young people growing up in Muslim families a greater sense of preparation for challenging distorted ideas should they come across them.

5. A sophisticated and fair mechanism of listening to communities; recognising that when power blocs within communities are pitted against each other – however much this may enhance the bargaining power of government – it can undermine trust and solidarity, not only in those communities but eventually in the wider society as a whole.

New Labour under Tony Blair made important strides in engaging Muslim communities (and faith communities more generally) by funding Muslim schools, opening up access to Whitehall, creating Muslim Peers and so on. These were significant steps for their time, now almost forgotten since our entry into Iraq and the 'war on terror'. Gordon Brown has showed a more nuanced understanding of the tensions in engaging with Muslims in a post-7/7 world. Further to this, the future must bring with it not only more representation on public bodies, knighthoods and grants, but also continued attempts to value the contributions of Muslims to British society, appreciate the serious tensions of leadership among Muslims and to empower communities through greater opportunities for education and the regeneration of neighbourhoods.

There is clearly a long way to go, but perhaps the starting point for Muslims is to give a greater sense of importance to domestic issues – the idea of the nation and belonging to it. This is not to say that the global is not important, but the British Isles are where 1.6 million Muslims and 59 million fellow citizens experience life, day in, day out. For the nation, the starting point could be to see that Muslims are really no different to other citizens. This is not about a clash of civilisations or even a clash of values; after all, much of what we all aspire to are basic human needs and desires. Think of freedom, equality, justice, accountable governance, rule of law, prosperity, education, charity, security: such values and notions have no single creed, no specific culture, and no particular civilisation. They are now truly universal and human aspirations.

Reference

The Runnymede Trust (1997) *Islamophobia: A Challenge for us All*. London: The Runnymede Trust

Hinduism

by Ramesh Kallidai, Secretary General, Hindu Forum of Britain

Hindus have been living in Britain since the 19th century. Hinduism received widespread attention in the Victorian era largely due to the work of the Theosophical Society and the emergence of Indology as a new field of academic study in British universities.

There have been three waves of migration of Hindus into the United Kingdom. The first wave began before India's independence in 1947 and continued until the 1960s. The economic conditions of that decade compelled many Indians to immigrate to the UK in search of greener pastures. The second wave occurred in the 1970s after Idi Amin, the Ugandan dictator, expelled Indians from his country. Thousands of Gujarati business persons who were British Overseas Citizens were forced to leave behind prosperous lives and migrate to the UK. The last wave of migration of Hindus to the UK began in the 1990s, and continues to this day. These migrants have mostly been Hindu professionals, including doctors and software engineers from India and political victims fleeing the ethnic conflict in Sri Lanka.

Today Hinduism is the third largest faith in Britain, with 750,000 followers in this country.[3] A key feature of the modern British Hindu community is that they are urban-dwellers, and scattered around metropolitan areas including London, Leicester, Birmingham, Manchester and Leeds. Although it is often thought that Hindus are usually Asian in origin, the 2001 Census highlighted the fact that 7,200 Hindus were white, 5,700 were mixed, 3,000 were Black and 3,000 were of other racial backgrounds.

---

3. The 2001 Census suggested that there are 559,000 Hindus in Britain. The figure of 750,000 was extrapolated by the Hindu Forum of Britain in 2007, based on immigration since 2001, and the number of Hindus who did not tick the faith box in the last Census.

The Hindu world-view of inclusion and respect is concisely defined by two principles enshrined in the *Rig-Veda*, one of the oldest books in the history of humanity. The first principle, known as *sarva-dharma-samabhava* (respect for all faiths), is captured in a *Rigvedic* verse that declares that there is one Truth, but the wise speak of it in different ways.[4] The second principle, *vasudhaiva kutumbakam*[5], declares that the whole world is but one unified family.

Arriving in a new country to settle down can be challenging: it can also provide opportunities. New Hindu arrivals faced their share of initial problems, including diet, climate, and acceptance into the host community.

Hindu parents, concerned to preserve their heritage, recognised the need to articulate teachings previously handed down by family and cultural tradition. Temples and religious groups established formal education classes, in language, scripture, and the performing arts. Despite the different appeals for continuity, the cultural aspects of Hinduism have, quite naturally, undergone significant changes. Young women are now less likely to wear traditional dress, and Hindu youth have developed their own brands of popular music.

In the 1970s, Hindus in the UK had begun to form festival committees to celebrate Hindu festivals including *Diwali* and *Navaratri*. As the community grew more affluent and settled into steady businesses and professions, the festival committees mushroomed into community organisations. Today there are over 400 Hindu organisations in the UK including national representative organisations such as the Hindu Forum of Britain and the National Council of Hindu Temples, and various regional organisations. There are also a range of community organisations based on social or linguistic identities that provide a wide range of services, as well as religious organisations and temples that provide religious and social support.

---

4. *Rig Veda*, Book I, Hymn 164, Verse 46: *ekam sad vipra bahudha vadanti*
5. *Maha Upanishad*, Verse 71: *Ayam nijah parovetthi gananam laghu-chetasaam udara charitanam tu vasudhaiva kutumbakam*; Translation: The petty minded see the world as 'this is mine and that is yours'. Those who are of noble consciousness however declare, 'the whole world is but a family'.

It would be hard to escape the Hindu influence on British society today in areas such as music, arts, diet, health and language. Hindu words such as 'pandit', 'pukka' and 'guru' are commonly used in everyday English. Indian cuisine is a cornerstone of the British diet and the curry has become an accepted British tradition and a common social ritual. Another popular Hindu 'offering' to British society is *yoga*, the ancient system of Hindu well-being. *Yoga* offers a holistic approach to body, mind and spirit, which provide people with the 'tools' to cope with the challenges of daily life.

There is strong evidence that Hindus have, by and large, integrated well into British society. A report published in July 2006, *Connecting British Hindus: An enquiry into the identity and public engagement of Hindus in Britain*, explored identity issues in the British Hindu community (Berkley 2006). It pointed out that Hindus are more likely to be married than the general population (60.8 per cent compared with 43.6 per cent), and less likely to be divorced (2.7 per cent compared with 8.1 per cent). Hindus are more likely than the average to own their own property and are less likely to reside in social or privately rented housing. The contribution of Hindu individuals to business and wealth creation in the UK has never been quantified but it is clear that there are many industrialists and business people from Hindu communities that have made a significant contribution (ibid). Similarly, in other professions such as medicine, accountancy and the law there are many members of Hindu communities making a significant contribution. More than one in three Hindus in employment is in professional or senior management positions.

In terms of some of the challenges facing the Hindu community, the *Connecting British Hindus* report highlighted the need for improved teaching about Hinduism in schools, monitoring of media stereotypes, dialogue with other faith communities (particularly Muslim minorities), and inclusion of the British Hindu experience in anti-racism work. Among 680 self-selected respondents to an online survey on the Hindu Forum of Britain website, about 75 per cent reported that they mostly or completely agreed with the statement 'I describe myself as a Hindu, rather than by my ethnicity.'

The Hindu Forum of Britain's response to the Commission of Integration and Cohesion's consultation in 2007 indicated that many Hindus are open to the idea of multiple identities. However, they do not believe that all cultures should be subjugated or assimilated into a single British identity. Forcing everyone into one homogenous unit that is a replica of the dominant culture will move the race and faith discrimination dialogue back by 50 years. For centuries, the British have been able to accommodate other identities, including Scottish, Welsh and English, without feeling the need to give up their British identity. Similarly, people of a particular ethnicity, faith, gender or age may develop feelings of belonging for a particular community and yet be equally comfortable about their Britishness. The notion that one can only be British if one gives up other identities is inherently flawed because multiple identities are a reality and a way of life. Public policy in Britain has largely been able to recognise the need for multiple identities and this is manifest in our equality legislation and good practices such as community consultation and equality impact assessments.

The question of identity and Britishness is often described in a Hindu context as a string of precious stones. Each precious stone is unique in its identity and different in colour. When exposed to different sources of light, each stone can change its hue. However, the stones are held together by a string that binds them into an object of utility and beauty. Similarly, there are different communities from diverse backgrounds that make up Britain. Within each community, a single individual can accept multiple and evolving identities under varying circumstances. The same person can be Hindu, Indian, British or a mixture of any combination of these, depending on a range of circumstances. But the one underlying principle that holds everyone together is their Britishness.

Britishness is an accepted way of life for most Hindus, especially since two-thirds of the community are British-born and identify themselves as British. The religious ethos in Hinduism fosters loyalty to the country of one's birth and residence almost as a religious obligation. A Hindu saying, *janani janma bhumishcha svargad api gariyasi*, declares that one's mother and motherland (the country of birth or residence) should be respected more than the heavenly realm itself.

The Hindu Forum of Britain's response to the Commission of Integration and Cohesion's consultation in 2007 indicated a growing feeling that the national debate surrounding multiculturalism needed to be replaced by a renewed focus on good relations. Multiculturalism often means different things to different people, with strong opinions favouring or opposing the notion of a multicultural society. The reality, though, is that there are diverse communities with varying cultural practices and different value sets living and interacting in Britain. Good relations based on equality, social justice, friendly interactions, conversations and dialogues can lead to greater cohesion and integration.

The role of public policy in making sure that diverse communities feel included in British life should not be diminished. The Hindu campaign to save Shambo the temple bull in Wales from slaughter highlighted this in a public manner. For Hindus who will not kill a cow under any circumstances, the fact that Shambo had Bovine TB was not a good enough reason to slaughter him. All life is sacred, according to Hindu doctrine. However, the Welsh Assembly Government had other concerns. They worried that the Bovine TB could spread to other herds in the area. Hindus reacted by providing bio-security measures to prevent the spread of the disease and appealed to uphold the sanctity of life in a Hindu temple. Although Shambo was eventually slaughtered, it did raise a national debate: should religious groups be given special privileges or exceptions from British law? Do such exceptions limit or reduce the notion of Britishness among such communities?

Many Hindus believed there were provisions in existing law that could have been used to prevent the slaughter of Shambo without seeking any special privileges. Practising their religion did not in any way limit or reduce their Britishness.

Several months after Shambo was killed, the RSPCA entered Bhaktivedanta Manor temple in Watford, and gave a lethal injection to kill a 'downer' cow (a live cow that cannot walk), Gangotri, that had been injured. The temple authorities claimed that one RSPCA member had distracted the temple farmer with a conversation while another slipped into the shed and administered the injection. The RSPCA denied this, saying that the cow was suffering and had to be put down. The temple believed that it had provided sufficient palliative care for the animal and their own vet had never made a professional recommendation to put the cow to sleep. They pointed out that killing downer cows had become an accepted practice only because most farmers did not have any economic incentive to take care of them. Cost was not an issue for the Hindu temple, however, and the RSPCA should have considered this. The Department for Environment and Rural Affairs eventually agreed to look at the care of temple animals and produce a protocol that would allow authorities to look at Hindu needs more sympathetically.

Shambo and Gangotri led many Hindu leaders to express a feeling that public policy has not been truly inclusive of the Indic-traditions (Hinduism, Sikhism, Buddhism and Jainism). They have expressed concerns that the four Indic faiths often seem to be an afterthought in public policy and interfaith dialogue, while there is a natural focus on the Abrahamic traditions due to historical affinity.

For instance, most hospitals or prisons in this country will easily cater to kosher or halal diets, but very few have the awareness of the requirements of a strict Hindu diet. Hindus are still unable to obtain coroners' certificates on the same day that a family member dies, while Jews and Muslims with similar funerary rules can easily do so. Animal welfare legislation includes provision for kosher and halal regulations, but does not provide for an understanding of the principles of ahimsa (non-violence) practised by Hindu temples that raise animals in their premises.

The *Connecting British Hindus* report stated that many Hindus in Britain felt isolated and excluded from the race dialogue in this country. At a Security Conference organised by the Hindu Forum of Britain in March 2007, Sir Ian Blair, then Commissioner of the Metropolitan Police, recognised this feeling in the Hindu community and assured them of measures to restore confidence levels.

But the Government needs to be cautious against the rolling out of public policy that can lead to segregation in the name of diversity, equality and cultural integration. In this context, the recommendations made in the *Cantle Report*, in the wake of disturbances in Bradford and Oldham, seem relevant. The report pointed out that housing and schools policies that favoured segregation in the name of cultural integrity and cohesion have had the unforeseen consequence of alienating the different religious, racial and cultural groups from one another.

However, the Hindu community in the UK continues to grow as one of the most integrated among the minority communities in the country. As Anthony Giddens, former Director of the London School of Economics, said in the *Guardian*, 'There are many different ethnic groups in Britain, and their fortunes vary. Those of Indian … origin are on average now outperforming the white population. They do better at school and their average level of income is higher. Intermarriage with other ethnic groups is rising steeply' (Giddens 2006).

In sum, it can be seen that the Hindu community is a firm and inherent part of British society. Britain is enriched by a range of different cultures, faiths, ethnicities and traditions. It is important that they are all supported in playing a fuller role in building a cohesive and integrated British society in which good relations between those who are different become the norm.

References

Berkeley R (2006) *Connecting British Hindus* London: Hindu Forum of Britain and Runnymede Trust
Giddens A (2006) 'Misunderstanding multiculturalism', *The Guardian*, October 14

Sikhism

by Dr Indarjit Singh OBE, Director, Network of Sikh Organisations

The Sikh community traces its history in Britain back to the nineteenth century. One of the first Sikh settlers in Britain was Maharaja Duleep Singh, son of the legendary Maharaja Ranjit Singh, 'lion of Punjab'. He was brought to Britain as a 16-year-old, following the English conquest of Punjab in 1849, and made to give up his Sikh faith, to which he later re-converted. He became a ward of Queen Victoria to whom he had earlier been 'persuaded' to 'give' the priceless Kohinoor diamond as a present. He spent most of his life in Thetford, Norfolk, vainly trying to return to and regain his kingdom in Punjab.

The early part of the twentieth century saw the arrival of a few Sikh students and professionals, as well as 'bhatras', itinerant traders. In 1908 the first Sikh gurdwara (temple) was established at Putney, Southwest London, soon moving to a building in nearby Shepherds Bush.

A seminal moment in Sikh history which impacted on the community in the UK was the partition of the Punjab, the homeland of the Sikhs, in August 1947. Tragically, with no time being given for an orderly movement of population, Sikhs in West Punjab had to flee their homes and hundreds of thousands were massacred. Many historic gurdwaras, including the birthplace of Guru Nanak, the founder of the Sikh faith, were now in the newly created state of Pakistan.

Overnight, a once prosperous and well-settled community became refugees. Despite incredible hardships, most resettled in places such as New Delhi and other parts of India, while others, particularly those who had seen armed service in Europe in the Second World War, migrated to other parts of the world. Many, lured by the post-war labour shortage, came to Britain, later bringing their families with them. In the 1960s, they were joined by a second wave of Sikh immigrants from East Africa fleeing new political turmoil, particularly that created by the regime of the Ugandan dictator Idi Amin. Now about 400,000 Sikhs live in Britain, mainly in its large cities. Wherever Sikhs have settled they have collected money to buy land to build a gurdwara or an old building that can be turned into one. There are now more than 200 gurdwaras in Britain.

Sikhs have always encountered problems due to ignorance and prejudice against their distinctive identity. In the 1950s and early 1960s, Sikhs with turbans found it difficult to work in transport and other public services. Children at schools experienced taunting and teasing, and not only from children. I was a witness in a libel trial in which a young Sikh boy coming to school for the first time wearing a turban was sent home by the head with the words 'it's grotesque, like something out of a pantomime; go home and remove it'. In the now celebrated Mandla case in the early 1980s, a Sikh boy was refused permission to go to school wearing a turban. The head teacher argued that it was religious discrimination, and not racial discrimination protected by the law. The case went all the way to the House of Lords, where in a historic ruling it was decided that Sikhs were protected by the Race Relations Act.

While the wearing of the Sikh turban is now better accepted in British society, ignorance still continues in places such as the USA, where two Sikhs were shot dead in the aftermath of 9/11. Even in Britain, turbaned Sikhs found themselves called 'Bin Laden'.

It is an interesting aside on the fickle nature of human behaviour that a distinctive Sikh identity, generally a focus for prejudice, is now applauded by thousands of cricket fans following the success of the England Sikh left-arm spinner Monty Panesar who was declared 'beard of the year' in 2006. Monty Panesar face masks enjoy huge sales in cricket grounds around the country.

There have been some changes in Sikh religious practice since their arrival in Britain. As Sunday is the traditional day of rest in Britain it is a convenient day for Sikh services at gurdwaras. There are, however, no hard and fast rules on this, and some congregations prefer Saturdays for the main service. If the celebration of a festival falls during the week, it is moved to the weekend. The religious processions, which are an important part of a festival in the Punjab, are less common here, and are generally confined to major areas of Sikh settlement.

There have been noticeable social changes in the Sikh community in the UK with the joint family system generally giving way to smaller nuclear families. Strong ties are still generally maintained with the wider family unit. The surrounding social environment has also had its effect, and marriage breakdown and divorce, which was rarely heard of among Sikhs, is sadly no longer a rarity.

As a result of the attack on the Golden Temple in Amritsar in 1984, many Sikhs fled Punjab, mainly to the UK and Canada as political refugees, some with eyewitness accounts of torture and suffering. In the UK, the result was a rapid growth of Sikh political organisations committed to righting the wrongs suffered by their brothers and sisters in India. But Sikhs were soon to learn a lesson in realpolitik, finding that no country was willing to risk trade and political influence in criticising the repression of Sikhs in the subcontinent. Political protest abroad got nowhere and effectively held back the involvement of UK Sikhs in British public life for nearly a generation.

Despite such setbacks, Sikhs have always taken a positive lead in building bridges with other communities. A Sikh contribution to the BBC Radio 4 feature 'Thought for the Day' in 1997 helped start a movement for an all-faith celebration of the Millennium and the creation of the Lambeth Group representing all faiths and meeting at Lambeth Palace to plan for this. The high points were the creation of a Faith Zone at the Millennium Dome and a highly successful Service of Reflection and Commemoration in the Royal Gallery of the House of Lords.

1999 saw the three hundredth anniversary of the founding of the Khalsa[6] in 1699. A huge celebration took place in London's Royal Albert Hall, attended by more than 5,000 Sikhs from all over the UK. Guests included the Prince of Wales, leaders of major faiths and of the main political parties. A similar event took place at the same venue in 2004 to mark the four hundredth anniversary of the first reading of the Sikh scriptures, the *Guru Granth Sahib*. This also was very much an inter-faith event with the same high profile of attendees and participants.

---

6. Khalsas are Sikhs who have undergone the sacred Amrit Ceremony initiated by the 10th Sikh Guru, Guru Gobind Singh in 1699.

The main representative body of the Sikhs is the Network of Sikh Organisations (NSO) with nearly 100 affiliated gurdwaras and other Sikh groupings. The NSO has developed links with most government departments and other statutory organisations and is playing a prominent role in ensuring that Sikhs play their full part in the life of the UK.

However, although the Sikh community is now playing an ever increasing role in British public life, problems remain, the most important being a sense of frustration among some that the community is frequently marginalised in public debate and in the distribution of resources. In addition, there is concern about the readiness of the media to champion the denigration of minority communities in the name of 'free speech'.

Sikhs have always championed the right to free speech: that is, the right to criticise those in positions of power or authority without the fear of, or regardless of, repercussions. Throughout its history, the Sikh community has played a heavy price for supporting this freedom. Sikhs do not, however, see free speech as the right to gratuitously insult others, as happened in Gurpreet Kaur Bhatti's play *Bezthi* ('Dishonour') in 2004, which featured rape, murder and foul language, set in a Sikh temple, and was advertised with a lurid poster depicting women's underwear. In the Sikh view this is not free speech; it is foul speech that shows no respect for others or for common decency. In putting the concept of free speech in its true perspective we would do well to be true to the words of the archetypal Englishman Rudyard Kipling when he wrote: 'Teach us the strength that can never seek, by deed or thought to hurt the weak.'

It is in public debate that Sikhs with egalitarian teachings have a potential to make a major contribution. Today the debate is about British identity. Some equate this with Christian teachings, or with a past culture, forgetting that culture is never constant. Sikh teachings suggest a need to look to a more inclusive identity, based on shared values. While Sikhs believe that we should show our loyalty and allegiance to the country we live in, this loyalty is not mutually exclusive to loyalty to Sikh teachings of respect for other faiths and other ways of life, concern with social justice and a fairer society. If Sikhs remain true to Sikh values, they will make an important and positive contribution to the life of this country.

Many words today are bandied about without any attempt at definition. 'Secularism' is such a word. A secular society is one in which no one religion imposes its values and beliefs on others, and this is something strongly supported by Sikh teachings. The word 'secularism' is, however, often used to suggest that religious beliefs and convictions have nothing positive to offer in our common quest for a more just society. This, in the Sikh view, is absurd. Values such as tolerance and respect, a recognition of the oneness of all humanity and a commitment to stand up to injustice whatever the cost, are central teachings of Sikhism, and their positive acceptance by all can only enhance society. Religion reminds us of the fallacy of the widespread belief that material wealth necessarily leads to happiness and contentment. Our common religious teachings, on the other hand, remind us that true contentment comes from looking outwards at the needs of others.

Closely linked to the word 'secularism' is yet another ill-defined 'ism': 'multiculturalism'. Sikhs believe we should be relaxed about different cultures existing side by side, providing this is not done in a spirit of exclusivity or superiority. We can all learn a lot from one another in a way that enhances our own way of life. There is, however, a very real danger of some people magnifying and exploiting superficial difference into something much more sinister. We should all be aware that ignorance leads naturally to prejudice, and prejudice can lead to hatred and violence. Today, the existence of different communities living together side by side is not a subject for academic debate; it is a reality of the world we live in and we all have a responsibility to make it work in a way that enriches us all.

Sikhs believe that our different religions are not all that different, and are in a way overlapping circles of belief. In that area of overlap, which is much greater than the smaller area of difference, we believe that we find common values of tolerance and respect, balance and responsible living, concern for others and a readiness to put the needs of others before our own. We believe that it is these values that should define British identity, and our overriding human identity.

Conclusion
Secular or sacred? Towards a new settlement between faith and the public realm

by Professor Michael Kenny

Some interesting points of agreement surface in the accounts offered in this collection of the history of the major faith communities in the UK. One is an appreciation of the capacity of British culture to allow space for very different religious traditions to flourish within it. Another is a sense that the 'settlement' that has evolved between state and Church in Britain has survived a number of challenges over the last few centuries. As some of the faith leaders here assert, a set of arrangements that grew out of the establishment of the Church of England have quietly adapted to allow recognition for a host of other denominations and non-Christian faiths.

These positive notes are intermingled with some critical references to experiences of intolerance and suspicion from the host culture, especially towards non-Christian traditions. And importantly this is not just an issue affecting the Muslim community. There is a tendency to overlook the difficult experiences that many Sikhs, Hindus and other 'world faiths' have had in securing recognition in Britain. Some worrying correlations persist between socio-economic inequality and religious background among different ethnic minorities in the UK, and pose important challenges for those committed to equality and social justice.

One further theme that arises in several of these contributions concerns a sense of unease with the multicultural framework which, some believe, has shaped how the political elite has responded to the multiplication of religions and cultures associated with inward migration over the last few decades. This has not, it is suggested, generated a durable framework for cultural integration and may have resulted in the tendency to treat cultural and faith groups as static silos, rather than dynamic communities possessing complex and changeable identities.

The place of faith?

What, then, are we to make of the mixed messages that these faith leaders provide about where religion fits into the national culture and identity of Britain?

On the one hand, we have their personal testimonies and considerable additional evidence to suggest that most members of religious groups do not feel that they are on the whole subject to unfair or arbitrary discrimination because of their beliefs or background.

On the other, there are indications that faith communities feel increasingly estranged from aspects of British culture. The reasons for this perception vary importantly between different communities. For many Muslims, worries about being framed as inveterate opponents of Western values and as potential security threats are paramount. For many Hindus and Sikhs, discomfort arises from a perception that their particular needs have been overlooked by the current focus on Islam, yet issues of socio-economic disadvantage and occasional cultural intolerance remain central. Christians, on the other hand, are animated by a different set of issues. Within the Church of England tensions between a growing evangelical current and an established liberal tradition are playing out over touchstone issues such as the ordination of gay members of the clergy, and are affected by wider debates in the international Anglican community.

These differences aside, there are also signs of a converging sense across these communities that the position of faith within the national public culture has become more marginal. This perception stems from a complex mixture of factors. These include: a recoil at what is perceived as the emergence of nakedly materialistic, hedonistic and narcissistic lifestyles and cultural values, especially among the young, fuelled by the affluent conditions of the 1990s; the decline of traditional family structures over the last two decades; the development of a media culture determined to break down taboos about sex and morality; the apparent weakening of the Christian influence in the UK, manifest in the falling number of congregants in the Church of England; and the steady secularisation of the national culture that has taken place over the last few decades.

A more recent cause of this growing sense of ennui is the perception that successive Labour governments, and state institutions more generally, have adopted a more determinedly 'faith-blind' approach in relation to the regulation of charitable activity and the provision of public resources. Labour's Human Rights Act extended the application of egalitarian principles, particularly for women, ethnic minorities and lesbians and gays, and has been regarded by some religiously-motivated people as representing a worrying infraction upon the rights of religious organisations to pursue their own convictions (even despite their entitlement to exemptions from some employment regulations).

This tension flared uncomfortably over the right of Catholic adoption agencies to turn away same-sex couples. A further ongoing source of strain between the religious and the predominantly secular values of the political class is associated with scientific developments in the fields of embryology and human reproductive technologies, and the efforts of government to provide an ethically robust framework for regulating research in these rapidly moving fields. The profound dilemmas raised by the creation of hybrid embryos and 'saviour siblings' now sit alongside abortion as enormously contentious moral issues, pitting some members of faith communities against the moral compass of the bulk of the political elite.

Another more recent development viewed by some in the world of faith as inherently threatening is the resurgence of a sharp-edged secularism associated with a variety of high-profile commentators (Martin Amis, Richard Dawkins, A.C.Grayling and Christopher Hitchens among others). This trend can to an extent be seen as a renewal of the nineteenth-century ideology of anti-clerical secularism (Keane 1999). While some of these arguments claim the mantle of the universalism of the Enlightenment, others suggest that the underlying bonds that provide the underpinnings of national identity are in essence secular, and view religious diversity as a potential threat to its coherence.

Faith and British values

This sense of estrangement is a growing concern not just for faith leaders: it has begun to move on to the agenda of policymakers and social commentators. Debates about Britishness, it has been suggested, provide one way of offsetting this growing sense of discord and disappointment. This is a stance associated with the Chief Rabbi, Jonathan Sacks. Along with the Head of the Equalities and Human Rights Commission, Trevor Phillips, Sacks has gained a wide hearing for the view that a rich sense of Britishness offers an appropriate framework for the integration of ethnic and religious minorities.

This is an important argument that deserves wider consideration across the communities of faith. But it should be seen as the beginning, not end, of the quest for a more robust and sinuous secular framework for shaping the relationship of state and faith. For there is a danger in open, mobile and dynamic societies that we promote and institutionalise too static and fixed an idea of national identity and culture. A more appropriate understanding of national identity in a society like Britain needs to allow room for a sense of the complex interweaving of indigenous and newer traditions and the establishment of important cultural hybrids that permit individuals to experience their sense of religiosity as nested within a broader sense of national belonging.

More generally, a successful national culture in a diverse and rapidly changing society needs to allow for a wide range of groups to see themselves reflected in its public expressions and cultural life, while remaining resolute about the governing ideals of its democratic inheritance – equality, citizenship, pluralism and tolerance. Just as important is the need for continual validation and celebration of the achievements bound up in the development of a secular public sphere, a development that provides the legal and moral preconditions for the exercise of religious conscience and expression, and that permits the exploration and promotion of non-religious ideas of 'the good'.

Striking the right balance between these cultural impulses and normative ideals is a process that may take more than one generation. Such an approach faces a major challenge from the rigid and dichotomous polarisation that afflicts debate about migration, citizenship and religion in Britain. In response to this frozen discourse, we need to reach beyond familiar orthodoxies about the need to separate faith and the public realm and lazy caricatures about the harms associated with religious practice. Such a shift of perspective is particularly overdue among political 'progressives', many of whom still take their bearings from the secularist ambition of removing religion from state and public square, and the unquestioned premise that religious belief is only ever a source of division within the body politic.

In the Anglo-American intellectual world, the seminal articulation of this position was provided by the major philosophical figure John

Rawls. His influential model of public reason (1993) led him to defend a sharp distinction between what he termed 'comprehensive' world-views, including religious ones, and the kind of secular reasoning that was likely to engage and persuade one's fellow citizens. Rawls's ideas have elicited sustained debate and much criticism among philoso-phers, including those as committed as he was to liberal values. Some have replied that attempts to keep arguments based on conscience and religious conviction out of the public square inherently discrimi-nate against those whose deep moral convictions inform their responses to questions of public policy and political life. Why, sceptics ask, should they not be permitted to bring to bear deeply held values and beliefs (religious or secular in inspiration) in the democratic conversation, so long as they abide by the procedural rules and egal-itarian values it requires (Taylor 2007)?

Whether the kind of faith-blind stance that Rawls promoted is viable in a world of interacting faiths, a rising interest in unconventional forms of spirituality, and a proliferation of ideas about what constitutes 'the good life', is now a major political as well as philosophical question. There is an overwhelming need in the UK for consideration of which kind of model is now most appropriate as a template for the regulation of the secular public sphere, and for the development of law and policy in the context of religious diversification.

The kind of faith-sensitive approach that philosophers such as Charles Taylor promote is still anchored in the values of democratic citizenship as the overarching regulative framework for the state's approach to people's personal beliefs and cultural identities. But it seeks to develop a more inclusive model of democratic dialogue – in which faith voices and deeply held values are not, as in the Rawlsian model, ruled out of order. It strives for a principled statement of the obligations and responsibilities of all citizens in a democracy, including those from faith backgrounds. Religious freedom is a cherished part of the value framework suggested by such a model, but is nested amidst a number of other freedoms and rights, such as freedom of speech, and these need to be balanced off against it.

The secular multi-faith state needs to become smarter and more sensitive about the harms and values associated with the faith communities dispersed throughout its social networks. And it should develop policy and law in this area within the parameters set by the principles of democratic citizenship. These require that all citizens are treated equally, irrespective of religion, race or gender, and that the state actively promotes a culture of equality and engaged citizenship among its population, and regards this last imperative as trumping demands for special treatment premised on cultural or religious tradition.

Towards the secular multi-faith state

Public debate about the legal and policy dilemmas associated with balancing these contending values needs to move up several gears if we are to find a principled and consistent way of dealing with the different areas in which faith surfaces as an issue of public significance in British society. And the development of such a discourse requires that three pressing challenges are addressed by stakeholders in this area.

The first of these involves the need for the state to acquire a better understanding of the contribution and place of faith in British society. Accurate, up-to-date information on the religious dimension of the most recent waves of migration is an important starting-point in this enterprise. There is a pressing case for more systematic and ongoing data-gathering about the plurality of faiths in the UK, and the myriad of activities, charities, voluntary groups and schemes that they promote, often for the public benefit. As a recent report examining the extensive contribution made by Christian charities in the UK has suggested, there are good reasons to think that authorities have underestimated the quantity of faith-based charitable endeavour, and that government is far from joined-up in its approach to the social benefits of faith activism (Davis *et al* 2008).

The inadequate mapping of the extent of religious involvement in social provision is a serious weakness given that there has been an important drift, largely below the radar of media attention and political debate, towards the greater involvement of such groups and organisations in providing schemes, services and opportunities for the non-religious in many different neighbourhoods and communities. More generally, given that the Conservative party has announced its intention to provide a greater and more autonomous role for the 'third sector' in delivering key public services, the question of what are the moral and legal implications of undertaking public services for religious groups and for the non-religious publics they may be serving is now a pressing one.

The second task follows directly from this and is of some urgency. We need to attune consideration of the role of faith in the public realm to the facts of their much closer cooperation and intersection. The idea of a clear and transparent divide between them, which figures so prominently in the contrarian arguments of both secularist and faith fundamentalists, has been overtaken by social practice. Numerous employers in the UK make allowances for the festivals and prayer times associated with their employees' faiths. Members of religious communities have over time been exempted from certain civil laws and can gain exemptions from aspects of the Government's equalities legislation. The state now sanctions and subsidises a variety of religious educational providers, Muslim schools included. Direct grants by the state to Islamic groups and faith groups more generally have multiplied in recent years. And different branches of government have been evolving ever closer relationships with congregations of various kinds (Norman 2008).

Public debate about the place of religion needs to catch up with these developments. Secularists are in effect arguing for a major severing of the tangle of relationships that have developed between religion and public life, and hope for a radical separation of the two that is not actually replicated in any other European state. Equally, those who complain about the hostility of government towards faith communities tend to underplay the amount of engagement with faith communities – Christian and Jewish, as well as Muslim – that the state has undertaken over the last decade. The drift towards closer relationships between faith and state is one good reason to jettison the ideal of faith-blindness and substitute it with an ethos more suited to a world of many faiths. Democracy's defenders now need a much more acute sense of the potential and problems that religion brings to the civic culture. British progressives in particular have good reason to take seriously the political scientist Robert Putnam's contention that religion remains one of the most reliable and impressive sources of social capital (Putnam 2000). Some of the recent initiatives launched by the Department for Communities and Local Government do suggest a growing recognition of the importance of faith-based social activism.

The third challenge that needs to be given more serious thought by politicians of all shades, as well as by faith leaders, concerns the impact of new forms of fundamentalism in the context of faith. The trends that have produced a growing sense of estrangement for some religiously-minded people have contributed to an atmosphere in which, in the most general terms, fundamentalist approaches of various kinds have flourished. While the current public focus is almost uniformly on radical Islam in this respect, there is a wider pattern, with important variations across different faiths, that has been overlooked. There is a Manichean quality to debates about the public role of religion which is conducive to a deepening intolerance on both sides. The seductively simple oppositions between 'Reason' and 'Faith', or 'Science' and 'Religion', which such thinking promotes, do enormous damage to our historical understanding and overlook the support that different religions have expressed for scientific discovery (Hind 2007). Some commentators, both atheist and religious in background, regard the promotion of a shrill and aggressive secularism is itself a manifestation of the more intolerant and polarised atmosphere that has developed of late.

Certainly within the major religious communities, tensions – and in some cases open conflicts – have become more acute between traditionalists and more moderate, modernist or liberal interpretations of sacred texts or tenets. One generic quality of religious fundamentalists is their opposition to the practice and ideals of religious pluralism. The development of a host of multi-faith projects and forums involving Christians, Jews, Muslims and Hindus among others, are not surprisingly major sources of fundamentalist ire.

The moral and strategic question of how to combat and manage the growing impulse to fundamentalism is one that engages leaders of all faiths. Yet little systematic or cooperative thinking has emerged on this score, despite the many important signs of multi-faith endeavour. Equally, the democratic state needs to take new kinds of fundamentalism much more seriously, and become more proactive in developing strategies to offset them. The promotion and institutionalisation of inter-faith cooperation, as well as faith and secular interaction, should be regarded as important tools in the struggle to combat fundamentalism. From this perspective, some important and contentious policy questions can be seen in a different light. The Government's recent promotion of multi-faith academies and argument that single faith schools broaden their intake (both controversial issues within various religious communities) might be seen as important elements in a broader anti-fundamentalist drive.

So, too, might a consideration of the *ad hoc* and fairly opaque institutional arrangements that exist for the interaction of government, politicians and faith communities. Do initiatives such as the Faith Communities Forum established by the Welsh Assembly, or Communities and Local Government's Faith Communities Consultative Council, work? Do they provide lessons and benefits that might be applied more widely? How should non-conventional 'faiths', and committed humanists, be represented on such bodies? These important questions have been buried in much of the progressive consciousness beneath a lingering fixation on disestablishment. A campaign for the latter, urged enthusiastically by some prominent liberal secularists, is far more likely to position the centre-left as a sectarian, intolerant force, obsessed with institutional tinkering rather than real issues. Far better to recognise that the creation of a healthy pattern of inter-faith dialogue and greater mutual respect among the faithful, as well as between believers and the secular-minded, are important goals for the democratic state, and issues much more likely to chime with public concern.

Such a framework is not without perils, and these need to be honestly discussed and carefully countered. In some instances, faith can be the source of considerable division, communal tension and intolerance; just as it can be an extraordinary force for social cohesion and justice. A faith-sensitive approach should not be regarded as necessarily a faith-sympathetic one. There is a risk, too, that if religion becomes a more salient category in the eyes of government departments and local officials, ethnic minority groups that are not aligned with a single religious tradition could disappear from public consciousness. And, more generally, advocates of the unique historical achievement and tremendous moral worth of the development of a secular public realm need to be clear that there are limits to religious freedom. The model of egalitarian citizenship that has animated the development of secular democracy requires that the state treats citizens as equal, irrespective of their cultures and religious beliefs. The stance of greater sensitivity to and engagement with faith outlined here must develop within such a framework, not in contravention of it.

But at a time when some of the powerful engines of social capital are weakening, and when many are disinclined to participate in conventional politics, there is a powerful argument for the state becoming more proactive in nurturing those communities where the internal voice of conscience engenders an altruistic imperative to engage positively with the social world. The potential of mobilisations from civil society, with religion as one of its main drivers, to inject a sense of impatience with current social arrangements into public discourse has been realised in movements ranging from Make Poverty History to campaigns against child poverty.

Faith sustains a complex web of identities, activism and well-being. It is now time for the democratic state to pay greater heed to the many different benefits and dysfunctions it brings to public life. And it is time as well for all of us to give greater attention to the actual and potential relationship of faith to British culture and community. Religion forms a central pillar of the story and development of Britishness. Ensuring that it remains a vital part of the nation's identity and social life, without encroaching on the hard-won freedoms and equality of Britain's citizens and values of the secular public realm, is a major challenge for policymaking at the start of the twenty-first century.

References

Davis F, Paulhus E, and Bradstock A (2008) *Moral, But No Compass: Government, Church and the Future of Welfare* Cambridge: Von Hugel Institute

Hind D (2007) *The Threat to Reason: How the Enlightenment was Hijacked and How we can Reclaim it* London: Verso

Keane J (2000) 'Secularism?' *Political Quarterly* 71, 1, pp 5-19

Norman ER (2008) 'Notes on Church and State: A Mapping Exercise', in

RM Morris (ed.) *Church and State: Some Reflections on Church Establishment in England* London: The Constitution Unit, pp 9-13

Putnam R (2000) *Bowling Alone: the Collapse and Revival of American Community* New York: Simon & Schuster

Rawls J (1993) *Political Liberalism* Irvington, NY: Columbia University Press

Taylor C (2007) *A Secular Age* Boston, MA: Harvard University Press